slash your MORTGAGE

HOME LOANS RIP-OFF EXPOSED

SAVE £000S OFF YOUR MORTGAGE

ROBIN BANKS

First published 1999

Kogan Page Limited
120 Pentonville Road
London N1 9JN

British Library Cataloguing in Publication Data

A CIP record for this book is available from the British Library.

ISBN 0 7494 3096 6

Typeset by Saxon Graphics Ltd, Derby
Printed and bound by Clays Ltd, St Ives plc

For Hannah and Kitty

Contents

Preface

Dear Homebuyer

The reward for just three hours' endeavour could be a once-in-a-lifetime family holiday, a smart new car, or sending your children safely through university. Or maybe all three!

Sounds incredible? That's because, if you're like most people, you've been conditioned to believe that mortgages are complicated and an unavoidable expense.

Well, you're in for a pleasant surprise. Mortgages are easy to understand. And, better still, you can achieve savings that run into tens of thousands of pounds using a few simple techniques that building societies and banks don't like to publicize.

Slash Your Mortgage is a no-holds-barred exposé of the lender's secrets and how you can beat their system. It challenges conventional mortgage 'wisdom' with simple logic. It maps out, concisely, how savings can be made both in the long and short term. And it guides you through the mortgage maze with seasoned advice.

I hope you find this book easy to read and easy to understand. Because the information it contains is of vital importance to you. What's more, it's your passport to remarkable savings. The only regret you'll have is that you didn't discover the lender's secrets sooner....

Robin Banks, June 1999

Introduction

Your golden nest egg is in your hands

This book is the best investment you'll ever make. Guaranteed. It shows you how to save many thousands of pounds on your mortgage now and *tens* of thousands of pounds in the future. It's based on fact, not fiction. And the techniques used are simple, safe and legal.

Understandably, many people in the United Kingdom won't want you to read this book. They belong to banks and building societies. Their reason? They stand to lose billions of pounds from people who work hard to own their home. And up until now they've been making a tidy profit by keeping you ill-informed, ill-advised and in the dark.

Now you can change that – it's quite literally in your hands. You'll discover within 30 minutes just how easy it is to make spectacular savings on your mortgage. Within one hour, you'll know how to select the best mortgage product that suits your budget. And within three hours, you'll have secured one of the safest, most profitable investments ever. And it may even cost you less than you're paying today.

This book gives you the facts you ought to know about, clearly and simply, to take advantage of the lender's 'loophole' and take control of your mortgage. Best of all, it's your shortcut to financial security. Don't miss this opportunity!

Three good reasons to take action

Big rewards, little effort

If someone offered you £1,000 for three hours' activity (nothing strenuous!) you'd be interested, right? And if that figure were increased to £20,000 for three hours' activity, you'd bite their hand off, wouldn't you?

Good! Because this book offers to do just that – by showing you how to slash thousands of pounds off your mortgage. *In just three hours!*

Here's how. First, spend an hour reading steps 1, 2 and 3 – that's 20 minutes per step (there's no gain without at least a little pain!). Next, pick up your telephone and contact a few lenders, then, later, fill in some paperwork (or get someone else to do it for you). That's another two hours' activity.

And that's it! There has never been a more financially rewarding three hours – unless you've already won the lottery! As the first person reading the manuscript for this book commented: 'This is the ultimate "get-rich-quick" scheme.' Pound per effort, it's certainly hard to beat.

A savings scheme with a tangible return

'Hatching your nest egg' will prove that you don't have to be a financial wizard to save an incredible sum of money. You'll discover that the techniques are simple and foolproof. And you'll save far more than you could ever hope to achieve compared to depositing savings each month in a bank or building society. Even reasonably 'safe' endowment policies can't match the returns you're about to witness.

You might argue that it's better to invest in the stock market rather than reduce your mortgage debt. If you're a risk-taker you *might* gain more. Nevertheless, as you'll also discover, even huge gains are worthless if you're paying off debt as well.

Clearing your mortgage debt is, quite simply, the safest investment you'll ever make. It's highly rewarding, too. And you won't be sinking your money into an investment that can go either up or down. For, reassuringly, this 'investment' can only go 'up'!

A question of loyalty

You've probably been with your present lender for years. And you haven't missed a mortgage payment. You even took out buildings and contents insurance with your lender because it told you how competitive it was. You've been loyal. And your lender has been very nice.

But when did you last receive a letter from your lender inviting you to take advantage of its special low interest deals? You've never received a letter?

That's because you're subsidizing your lender's low interest deals. And they're offered to first-time buyers with no track record of making even one mortgage payment. Even those remortgaging with your lender get a better deal than you do. Is your lender being loyal to you?

Retailers, supermarkets, petrol stations and insurance companies – to name a few – have loyalty schemes. They recognize you have a choice. So they use bonus points, stamps, even reduced premiums (horror!) to reward your continued custom. That's loyalty.

Mortgages work in reverse. It's the only business that penalizes you for loyalty. So much for loyalty!

And lastly...

If you don't already have one, you'll need a calculator. You don't need a multifunction, all-singing all-dancing one; a basic calculator with a [%] key will do. You'll get one for under £5.

STEP 1

Between a rock and a hard place?

Making sense of your mortgage, how it works, and why one repayment method can save you thousands

First things first

So, what is a mortgage? It is simply a loan of money to finance the purchase of your home. Your home acts as security for the repayment of the loan; in other words, it is a secured loan. If you fail to make regular payments, the lender has the right to repossess your house and sell it to recoup the outstanding balance on the loan.

This right is secured by registering a charge in the District Land Registry (Land Register in Scotland). Any additional loan that is secured to your house is also registered as a charge.

When you sell your house, the charge must be removed before your house changes hands. The charge can only be removed when you repay the sum owed on your mortgage to the lender(s).

Repayment of the mortgage is typically spread over 25 years. And when the loan is finally repaid, you have full legal title to your home and you're a homeowner.

Interest is profit

The lender's reason for offering mortgages is to make profit. It's a lucrative business. How much profit the lender makes is largely determined by the interest it charges to borrowers, offset by the interest it gives to savers. This differential is usually in the region of between 1.5 and 4 per cent.

It doesn't sound very much, but don't forget that there are huge sums of money involved. Some lenders' profits are in excess of a colossal £2 billion. Little wonder chairmen's salaries are usually £300,000-plus a year!

Also, although most of the lender's funds are withdrawable on demand or at short notice, the lender will still be investing savers' money at a higher rate than it gives in return, hence adding to the profit it makes from mortgages.

Naturally, the lender must make a reasonable profit from your mortgage or it wouldn't be able to provide the service. But what is a reasonable profit? 100 per cent? 200 per cent? 300 per cent? You're about to find out.

Why MIRAS isn't such a great deal today

Government help with your mortgage comes in the form of the Mortgage Interest Relief At Source (MIRAS) system. It was first introduced in 1983 as a financial incentive to encourage home ownership. It ends in April 2000.

Currently, providing you pay income tax, you receive tax relief on the interest paid to the lender on the first £30,000 of your mortgage loan. If your loan is more than £30,000, the portion above this threshold doesn't qualify for tax relief and you pay interest at the full rate. Tax relief is deducted by the lender so that your monthly payments are net of tax relief.

The amount of tax relief has reduced since it was first introduced and currently stands at 10 per cent. Table 1.1 shows the effect of MIRAS on your monthly payment and why, as interest rates fall, it's not the great tax saving it once was.

Table 1.1 *Amount of monthly MIRAS relief on a 25-year loan of £30,000*

Interest Rate	Monthly Saving (Interest-only)	Monthly Saving (Repayment)
15%	£37.50	£34.39
14%	£35.00	£31.65
13%	£32.50	£28.93
12%	£30.00	£26.22
11%	£27.50	£23.55
10%	£25.00	£20.90
9%	£22.50	£18.31
8%	£20.00	£15.79
7%	£17.50	£13.35
6%	£15.00	£11.01
5%	£12.50	£8.78
4%	£10.00	£6.69
3%	£7.50	£4.76
2%	£5.00	£2.99
1%	£2.50	£1.40

Since MIRAS ends in April 2000, all calculations in this book will assume MIRAS has already been scrapped. This will make the figures more realistic since this book deals with the future, not the past. Enjoy MIRAS while it lasts!

Interest-only vs repayment

There are two methods to repay your mortgage. One is interest-only – also known as endowment, PEP (personal equity plan) or pension; the other is repayment – also known as capital and interest, capital repayment or annuity.

Argument as to which method is best has been going on for years. Even the Office of Fair Trading can't agree. In the past, it has criticized lenders and independent financial advisers (IFAs) for recommending interest-only mortgages; and barely a year later, it has advised borrowers to think twice before entering a repayment mortgage. (The reasons are explained shortly.)

If the Office of Fair Trading is confused, what chance for the layperson?! However, as you're about to discover, one costs significantly more over the term.

Bad choice

The most common mortgage in the UK today is the interest-only method. Usually an endowment, PEP (now individual savings account, ISA) or pension-linked policy runs in conjunction with the mortgage. This is the investment plan that is used to repay the loan at the end of the term.

If you chose this method to repay your mortgage, it's probably because it appeared to be the least expensive arrangement. Or maybe it was the lure of a large lump sum paid to you when the investment plan matured – in effect, combining saving with home-purchase.

For whatever reason (and hindsight is a luxury!) it certainly looks more attractive, but, as you'll see later, appearances are deceptive.

If you were persuaded into this arrangement, here's why: there are fat commissions paid to lenders and IFAs who sell these plans, particularly 25-year endowment policies. Is it a coincidence that interest-only mortgages were routinely sold in the 1980s – which just happened to coincide with the growth in home ownership?

No guarantees

The problem with some interest-only mortgages is that there are no guarantees that the balance of the mortgage will be repaid from the profits of the savings plan. (Not that the IFA who sold you the plan cares – commissions are generally paid out from your first two years' monthly instalments.)

This is true of the popular 'low-cost' endowment, PEP and pension plan. If the investment plan matures and the profits are far more than were projected, you and the IFA simply got lucky.

On the other hand, you may well receive a letter from your investment company asking you to purchase another investment policy or increase your monthly payments. This is because projected profits at maturity look likely to be below the sum required to repay your loan.

One of the reasons for this is that the original projections were unrealistic for today's climate of low growth and low inflation. For endowments, average annual growth is quoted at 7.5 per cent (May 1999) rather than the previous 10 per cent. This is due to a sustained fall in interest rates, which has lowered the projected returns from equities (stocks and shares), bonds and gilts – resulting in lower returns on the money invested on your behalf. Reducing quoted average annual growth to around 6 per cent is already in the pipeline.

It is important to remember that you are liable for any shortfall at the end of the mortgage term, not the life assurance company. So, keep an eye on the progress of your repayment vehicle. It's more important than most people give it credit for.

Good choice

Less common nowadays is the repayment method, mostly for the reasons why interest-only mortgages are now so prevalent!

During the 1970s and early 1980s, however, this was the most popular method of repaying a mortgage, accounting for almost 70 per cent of all mortgages in 1978. Of course, there are drawbacks too, particularly in the way some lenders calculate interest on the loan. But in the main, this method is the safest, cheapest and most flexible route to repaying your mortgage.

Interest-only mortgage

This type of mortgage requires that you pay only the interest on the loan over the term. Your monthly mortgage payments only change when interest rates rise and fall.

The capital you originally borrowed is repaid at the end of the term as a lump sum, funded from the proceeds of an endowment policy, PEP or pension-linked plan.

This type of mortgage benefits not just the commission-driven IFA but lenders too. Why?

Since there are no capital payments made over the duration of the mortgage, the loan balance remains unchanged throughout the mortgage life. In short, the lender gets maximum interest over the whole term.

If the interest rate stays at 10 per cent for the full term, how much interest do you think you'll pay over 25 years? For a £50,000 mortgage (ignoring MIRAS), you'll pay back a whopping £125,000 in

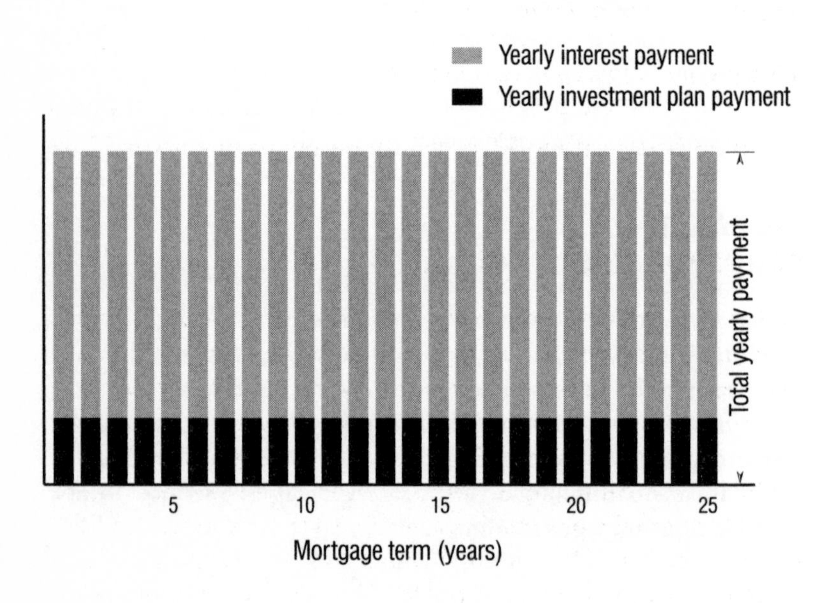

The illustration above assumes interest doesn't change over the full term. In reality, your monthly interest payments will go up and down in line with the lenders interest rates. Your monthly investment premium, however, remains fixed throughout the term.

Figure 1.1 *How your interest-only mortgage works*

interest. And you still have to pay back the £50,000 you originally borrowed. That's £175,000 in total.

That's the equivalent of 250 per cent profit to the lender. Justifiable?

Another little 'quirk' with interest-only mortgages is that some lenders charge a slightly higher interest rate compared to their capital repayment counterpart. This is typically between 0.25 and 0.75 per cent more. The reason, apparently, is that lenders have to wait longer to get their money back!

Calculating your monthly payment

Say you have a £60,000 interest-only mortgage and the interest rate is 8 per cent, your monthly premium is:

£60,000 × 8% ÷12 months = £400

(If MIRAS had been included, your monthly payment would be £380.)

Your repayment vehicle

On top of your interest payments, you must also pay an insurance premium every month towards a tax-free investment plan: an endowment, PEP or pension-linked scheme. This is the vehicle that repays the original loan back to the lender. Most common is the endowment; however, they all work on the same principle.

The investment plan runs for the term of the mortgage. At the end of the term the plan matures, yielding a tax-free lump sum that is used to repay the debt owed to your lender. Any surplus is yours.

Your monthly payment, pooled with those of other plan members, is invested in the stock market. The performance of the stock market is linked to how well your investment plan performs, and how much you receive at the end of the term.

Maturity values from endowment policies and pension plans are now spiralling downwards; PEPs have been replaced by untested ISAs. However, don't worry! Using the technique in Step 2, you'll find that any anxiety about maturity values will be over how much extra you'll get back rather than how to finance a shortfall.

Endowment policies

Endowment policies are made up of three elements: a 'sum assured' that the insurer promises to pay at maturity; 'annual (reversionary) bonuses' that once allocated can't be taken away; and a 'terminal bonus', paid at the discretion of the insurer when the policy matures, which can be as much as 50 per cent of the fund's final payment.

This structure is designed to smooth out the peaks and troughs of the stock market so that, should the stock market crash just before the policy matures, accumulated bonuses ensure a reasonable payout.

Life assurance companies approach the bonus structure in different ways. Some, as a deterrent against early surrender, offer lower annual bonuses but a high terminal bonus at the end of the investment term. Others offer higher annual bonuses but a lower terminal bonus. Whatever way they use, the investment's performance depends on the ability of the fund manager(s). Actual performance, therefore, is unpredictable.

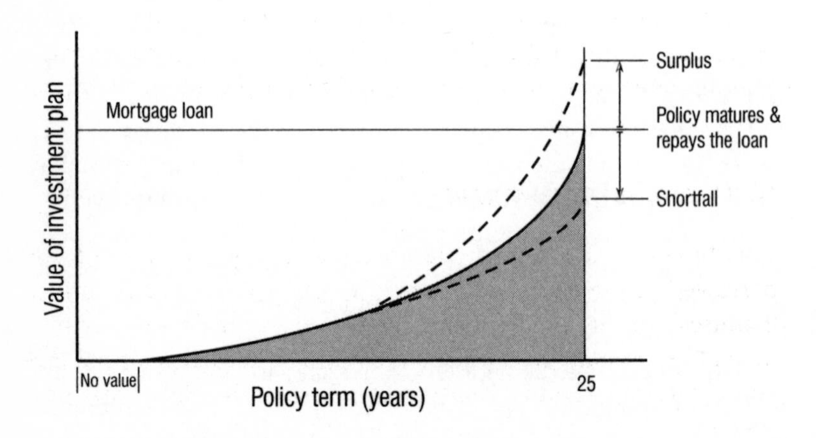

Figure 1.2 *How your investment plan works*

As well as paying off the capital sum at the end of the mortgage term, an endowment policy also provides you with life cover. This means that if you die during the term of the policy, the life assurance company agrees to pay out the full amount of the original mortgage loan.

What about surrender values? In the first two years, there's little or no surrender value; from two to seven years, you'll receive less that you put into it. What's more, you could be liable for tax if you surrender early. If you must surrender, wait until the next annual bonus has been allocated. An alternative is to sell or auction your policy. You could well get more than the surrender value but the policy usually has to be at least seven years old before it's considered. And don't forget, the purchaser will receive the full value of the policy if you die during the term. If you desperately need a cash injection, you can borrow from the life assurance company using the policy as security. Interest rates are typically lower than those of the High Street banks.

There are four different types of endowment policies that can be used to repay a mortgage. It's worthwhile checking to see what type you have.

Non-profit (or 'guaranteed') endowment

This type of endowment guarantees to repay the amount you borrowed at the end of the term. It doesn't pay out any extra. Monthly premiums are expensive, and the policy is generally poor value.

'With-profits' endowment

This type of endowment guarantees to repay the amount you borrowed at the end of the term, plus some extra money termed 'bonuses', 'profits' or 'dividends'. How much extra depends on how much the company decides to store up for you each year and give you as a terminal bonus. This type of policy has the highest monthly premium.

Low-cost (or 'build-up') endowment

This type of endowment is a 'with-profits' policy. It doesn't, however, cover the original amount you borrowed from the lender. The idea is that yearly bonuses build up so that by the end of the term, you have enough to repay the loan and (hopefully) collect some extra for yourself. Monthly premiums are obviously less than those for a full 'with-profits' policy or non-profit policy. This is the most common type of policy.

Unit-linked policies

This is a derivation of the endowment scheme. However, unlike a 'with-profits' endowment that can only go up or stay static, the value of a unit-linked fund can go up and down. Premiums are flexible; they can be increased to buy more units, or reduced to buy fewer. Also, since there is no set maturity date, you can defer selling units until their value is sufficient to repay your mortgage loan, or you can pay off your mortgage loan early. The final lump sum is tax-free and the policy has built-in life cover. Monthly premiums are on a par with a low-cost 'with-profits' policy and can provide a higher rate of return.

PEPs

Personal equity plans (PEPs) work in the same way as endowment plans. You make monthly payments to the lender to pay the interest on the mortgage loan, and a separate monthly payment to the PEP provider who invests your money in the stock market. PEPs have since been replaced by ISAs. So, although your PEP remains intact, your plan provider will now be investing your monthly premium in an ISA plan.

The value of the PEP (and ISA) can rise or fall, and being higher risk than an endowment policy, it offers a higher return. But, as there is no set maturity date, you'll have to wait until the value of the plan is sufficient to repay your mortgage loan. Bear in mind that there's no guarantee that this will happen. On the other hand, if your plan performs well, you could pay off your mortgage loan early.

The lender also requires that a separate level term life assurance policy be taken out for the full amount of the loan. This is to ensure the mortgage is repaid in full in the event of your death.

Pension-linked plans

Pension plans also work in the same way as endowment and PEP plans. You make monthly payments to the lender to pay the interest on the mortgage loan, and a separate monthly premium that's used to repay the mortgage loan and provide you with a pension on your retirement.

Only 25 per cent of the pension fund can be taken as a tax-free lump sum. And since part of the fund is used to repay the mortgage loan, you'll not only have a reduced future income, it's also taxable. If you're in this position, Step 2 will show you how to eliminate this potential problem.

As with PEP mortgages, the lender also requires that a separate level term life assurance policy be taken out for the full amount of the loan. This is to ensure the mortgage is repaid in full in the event of your death.

Home-equity plans

This type of plan uses the equity tied up in your home, though it's only available to those approaching, or over, retirement age. An interest-only loan or lump sum is provided by the lender, with which you buy a purchased life annuity from the lender. This provides a guaranteed regular income for life. Fixed mortgage payments are made to the lender to pay only the interest on the mortgage loan; the loan is repaid on the death of the borrower – either from the proceeds of the estate of the borrower or on the sale of the property. Only a few lenders, however, offer this loan facility.

Repayment mortgage

This type of mortgage requires that you pay both the interest and the capital on the loan over the term. Your monthly mortgage payments only change when interest rates rise and fall.

The capital you originally borrowed is repaid throughout the term. Part of each monthly payment represents interest on the amount still owed; the rest goes towards repaying the loan.

In the first years of your mortgage most of the monthly payment is interest, with a very small part capital. As the years go on, the amount you owe reduces, and therefore, the amount of interest that's charged on the outstanding loan is less.

So, how does the lender win with this type of mortgage scheme?

First, very little of your monthly payment is applied to repaying the loan in the first 10 years. Indeed, you only own 17 per cent of your home 10 years into the loan, and only 57 per cent of your home

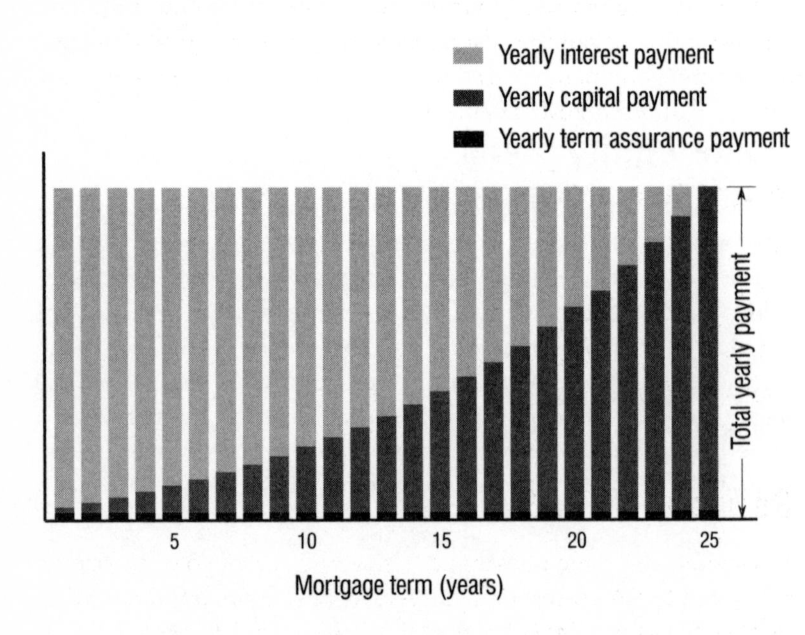

Figure 1.3 *How your repayment mortgage works*

20 years into the loan. If you sell your house or lose it during this time, you still owe the lender the bulk of the loan.

Second, depending on how the lender calculates the interest on the loan, you could pay interest on money you have already paid the lender – for a whole year! This was highlighted in the BBC consumer programme *Watchdog* in October 1998.

This is how it works: Say you take a loan of £50,000 and interest rates remain at 10 per cent throughout the first year. Interest for the first year is £5,000. Your payment is £459 per month. At the end of the first year the lender deducts your first year's payments (£459 × 12 = £5,508) from the outstanding balance of £55,000 leaving a balance at the end of year 1 of £49,492 (in effect you have reduced your loan by £508).

Each payment that's made makes no difference to the amount of interest you are charged until the end of the year. That's a whole year's worth of payments making money for the *lender* before your loan is reduced.

This scheme is called 'annual rest'. Not all lenders calculate interest this way, but the vast majority do (see Appendix A for a list of lenders who operate this scheme, and those who operate 'daily rest' and 'monthly rest' schemes).

Your life cover

On top of your capital and interest payments, you must also pay an insurance premium every month to ensure that the outstanding capital is repaid in the event of your death. This type of insurance is called 'decreasing term' life assurance and is relatively inexpensive, around £10 per month for £50,000 cover. You don't get anything back at the end of the term, however.

Reduced MIRAS

You should also remember that as the capital part of your loan drops below the MIRAS threshold, you receive relief only on that portion that qualifies for it. MIRAS, however, ends in April 2000.

Calculating your monthly payment

Refer to Appendix B for details on how to calculate your monthly payment easily for a comprehensive range of interest rates. Remember to use your original mortgage term (for example, 25 years) as the term remaining and your original mortgage loan when calculating your new monthly payment as from April 2000.

The catch

Interest-only or repayment? Which method is the better option? The most compelling reason for choosing a repayment mortgage over an interest-only mortgage is down to one factor: interest savings.

No matter what the interest rates are, or how much you borrowed, the fact is that you simply don't pay back as much interest over the term with a repayment mortgage compared to an interest-only mortgage. Check out the graph in Figure 1.4.

Don't forget this graph is only comparing interest payments – capital payments, investment plans and term assurance policies are excluded.

The difference is staggering!

Do you want to know the difference in interest charges between the two? Let's compare both types of mortgage over 25 years. Assume that the original amount borrowed is £50,000 and that the interest rate never varies from 9 per cent over the term.

For the interest-only mortgage, your monthly payment would be £375 and the total interest paid over the term is £375 × 12 months × 25 years = £112,500.

For the repayment mortgage, your monthly payment would be just under £425. You'd pay £127,500 over the term (£425 × 12 months × 25 years) but you've also repaid the capital. Deduct the £50,000 capital and this leaves the total amount of interest paid over the term, which is £77,500.

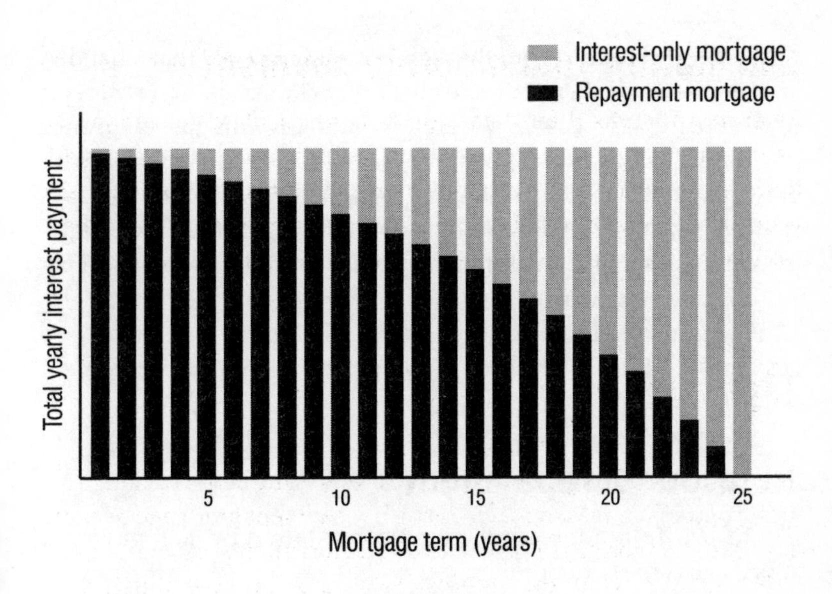

Figure 1.4 *Comparing total yearly interest payments*

The difference in interest payments to the lender is an incredible **£35,000**. That's the equivalent of just over **£116** a month extra in interest you'll pay on an interest-only mortgage.

Moreover, an interest rate of 9 per cent is fairly conservative. The average interest rate over the past 10 years has been over 11 per cent.

In defence of interest-only?

Of course, this example compares only interest payments. There's still the £50,000 owed to the lender.

The monthly payment for the interest-only mortgage is obviously lower than the repayment mortgage since the latter includes capital payments. In all probability, the type of investment plan used to repay the interest-only mortgage means you won't pay the £50,000 out of your own pocket. Rather, you'll pay around £30,000 (typically £100 per month) towards the plan with the remainder made up by the investment company growing your fund.

At the end of the term, though, it is your £50,000 that's handed over to the lender. Only the surplus is yours to keep. And neither is guaranteed. Worse still, when you add in both life assurance premiums to the mortgages, you'll save around £40 a month with the repayment method. Calculate that over 25 years and you save another £12,000. The difference is now a hefty **£47,000** between the two mortgage types (assuming the investment plan repays the loan in full, no more, no less).

If you have an interest-only mortgage, would you like to pay less interest and keep more of the profits from your investment fund?

In favour of repayment

There are four more indisputable reasons why a repayment mortgage is the better option.

Building equity

The first is that you build equity from your home faster. This means that as your property rises in value, and the amount you borrowed decreases, the more you own of your property. The more you own, the more 'equity' you have.

Put more simply, should you need a large sum of money, such as for home improvements or consolidating debt, you have a ready source of funds at your disposal. You can access this money either by remortgaging or by taking out a second mortgage (an equity-release loan).

Alternatively, should you move, you can put a bigger deposit on your new home. Doing so usually means you qualify for lower interest rates and better terms with the lender. In addition, you'll be able to borrow more from the lender, enabling you to move up to higher-value property faster.

You've made a profit

Second, you may have paid less for your house than perhaps it is actually worth. For example, assuming the value of your home was £50,000 when it was originally purchased and house prices triple over the term, your home would be now worth £150,000. Using the example on page 18, you would have made £22,500 profit (£150,000 – £127,500) using the repayment method, rather than a £12,500 loss (£150,000 – £162,500) using the interest-only method.

Flexibility

Third, repayment mortgages are more flexible. If interest rates rise and you find it difficult to meet your monthly mortgage payment, you can extend your mortgage term rather than pay out more each month. This process absorbs the rate increase by spreading payments over a longer period.

Interest-only mortgage payments are tied to the prevailing interest rate, so no matter how many years you have left to pay on your loan, your interest payment is always the same.

Furthermore, you can't adjust your monthly investment plan payment as this is fixed from the outset.

The end of MIRAS

Fourth, MIRAS benefits the interest-only mortgage more than repayment since the loan balance remains unchanged and maximum relief is applied throughout the term. MIRAS is scrapped in April 2000. So, although everyone loses when the tax benefit disappears, interest-only mortgages are worse hit.

Interest savings

Table 1.2 shows you just how much interest you would save with a repayment mortgage for various amounts borrowed at interest rates of 14 per cent, 11 per cent, 8 per cent and 5 per cent over 25 years. Remember, the average interest rate has been 11.2 per cent over the past 10 years.

Table 1.2 *Interest savings with a repayment mortgage*

Loan	14%	11%	8%	5%
£100,000	£86,254	£78,149	£65,803	£47,619
£95,000	£81,941	£74,242	£62,513	£45,238
£90,000	£77,629	£70,334	£59,223	£42,857
£85,000	£73,316	£66,427	£55,933	£40,476
£80,000	£69,003	£62,520	£52,642	£38,095
£75,000	£64,690	£58,612	£49,352	£35,714
£70,000	£60,378	£54,705	£46,062	£33,333
£65,000	£56,065	£50,797	£42,772	£30,952
£60,000	£51,752	£46,890	£39,482	£28,571
£55,000	£47,440	£42,982	£36,192	£26,190
£50,000	£43,127	£39,075	£32,902	£23,809
£45,000	£38,814	£35,167	£29,611	£21,428
£40,000	£34,502	£31,260	£26,321	£19,048
£35,000	£30,189	£27,352	£23,031	£16,667
£30,000	£25,876	£23,445	£19,741	£14,286
£25,000	£21,563	£19,537	£16,451	£11,905

The real cost of your mortgage

It is important to realize that the amount you borrowed from your lender is simply your mortgage loan. It's not what you'll pay back over the term. The amount you pay back over the term is your *real* mortgage.

Bear in mind that it's not only about comparing the monthly payments between the two types of mortgage and using this as the yardstick. It's about interest payments, interest rates and whether the lender calculates interest payments using the annual rest, monthly rest or daily rest accounting method too. They all contribute to the total expenditure on your home over the term.

Also, mortgages have changed out of all recognition over the past 25 years. And taking advice from your 'elders' is not the route to saving money! Even worse is that lenders and mortgage advisers are still misleading borrowers with false (deliberately or otherwise) and inadequate information.

Clearly, the repayment method is the most cost-effective and safest way to finance a mortgage. The only way an interest-only mortgage gains is when the investment plan grows significantly year on year and inflation remains low. This scenario reduces the risk of inflation eating away the profits of the investment plan. Unfortunately, it's not a realistic scenario with interest rates predicted to remain low for a long time.

Treat your mortgage as you would any investment. It's a very profitable investment and very low risk; few investments can boast that – ask any financial adviser! But it's only a profitable investment if you don't pay over the odds for it.

Now, in Step 2, you'll discover how to save thousands of pounds on your mortgage – be it repayment or interest-only – using techniques that are often overlooked and, curiously enough, not publicized!

STEP 2

Hatching your nest egg

Exploiting the lender's 'loophole' that guarantees to save you tens of thousands of pounds in the long term. The question is, how much do you want to save?

It's an old cliché, but buying your home is probably the largest investment you'll ever make. So, when you first took out your mortgage, did you find out how much you'd ultimately pay over the term? Sure, you can afford the monthly payments. But the true cost of buying your own home doesn't bear thinking about, does it?

You're not alone. It would seem there is no obvious alternative to paying what the lenders demand. However, as you're about to discover, there is a guaranteed way of saving a major slice of the lender's pie for yourself. In fact, you'll be able to turn the tables on the lender and make buying your home one of *your* best investments, rather than the *lender's* best investment.

So, get your calculator, pen and paper ready and discover how to secure your long-term financial future without actually working for it....

But what about all the calculations?

Don't be intimidated by all the numbers you're about to come across. They're derived very simply and you only have to understand the very basics of arithmetic to calculate them. As a quick demonstration:

If you pay £250 a month on your mortgage, how much would you pay over 20 years assuming your payment stayed the same? The answer is £250 × 12 months × 20 years = £60,000. Easy, wasn't it?

Now, how much would you pay a month on a £60,000 interest-only loan at an interest rate of 8 per cent over 18 years? Again, the calculation is simple: £60,000 × 8% (remember to press the [%] key) ÷ 12 months = £400.

What about the 18 years? Don't forget that with an interest-only loan, it doesn't matter if you've only one year or as many as 30 years left of the term, your monthly payment will always be the same.

On the other hand, the term remaining on a repayment mortgage *is* important. To calculate your monthly payment for the example above, refer to Appendix B, page 120. For a repayment term of 18 years, multiply the cost per £1,000 corresponding to 8 per cent (that is, 8.8918) by 60. Make sure you get £533.51.

And that's about as hard as it gets! In the interests of readability, all monthly payments are rounded up to the nearest £1 (so the above £533.51 will be rounded up to £534), and total mortgage costs and savings are rounded down to the nearest £10.

Now, take a deep breath....

Back to basics

So, what is your mortgage? It's the amount you will pay back to the lender over the full term of your mortgage loan. In other words, it's *not* what you borrowed. Check out the two graphs in Figure 2.1. The graph on the right is what you'll achieve by taking advantage of the

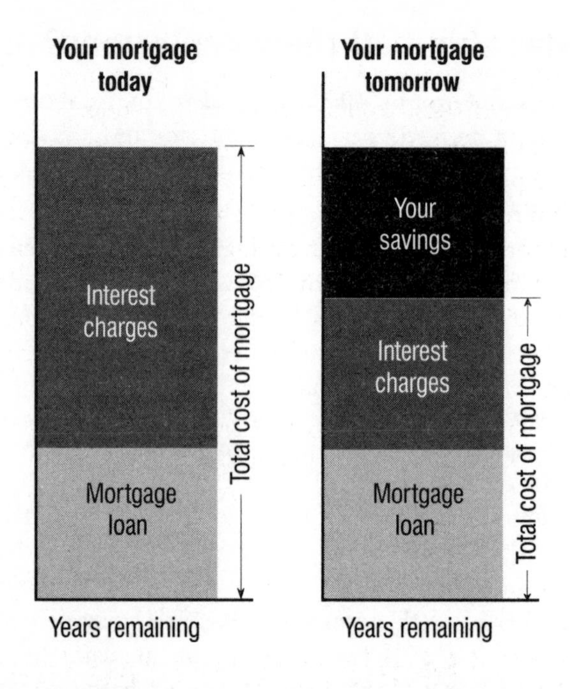

Figure 2.1 *How much can you save?*

lender's 'loophole'.

Of course, there's no way you can determine how much you'll finally pay over the term (unless you took out a 25-year fixed rate deal). The reason is that it's all down to fluctuations in interest rates over the duration of your mortgage loan. And the higher the interest rate, the more you'll pay.

Your first goal, therefore, is to make sure that you pay as little interest as possible on your mortgage loan over the mortgage term. Which means taking as many low interest-rate deals as often as you can. This is covered in Step 3 but just to illustrate this point, let's assume that you've paid off your mortgage loan of £50,000. Let's also assume that you never took a special low interest-rate deal over the term, resulting in an average interest rate over the 25 years of 11 per cent.

If you had taken an interest-only mortgage, your mortgage payment on average would have been £458 per month. This would mean a total of £137,400 paid in interest to the lender.

Just suppose instead you had remortgaged every five years, securing a 3 per cent discount for two years in each of the five-year periods. You're *average* interest rate will have dropped to 9.8 per cent. And your mortgage payment on average would have been £408 per month, a saving of **£50 per month**. This would have resulted in a total of £122,400 paid in interest to the lender, a saving of **£15,000**.

Using the same analogy, you would have saved nearly £13,000 with a repayment mortgage.

As you can see, the lower the interest charged on your mortgage loan, the less you will pay back to the lender. Guaranteed.

This is the first step to saving you thousands. There are two more to come...

What the lenders don't tell you

The second step is taking advantage of the lender's 'loophole'. It's an open secret; the lender will tell you if you know what to ask. But it's likely that you've neither had the inclination to, nor realized the consequences of one of the lender's less publicized policies. But it's available to every homebuyer who wants to cut his or her debt and profit from home ownership.

The fact is that lenders allow you to repay your mortgage loan using both the interest-only method and the repayment method – a sort of 'mix and match' mortgage. Not exactly an overwhelming statement perhaps. Indeed, you may already know about it. But consider the implications.

If your current mortgage loan is for £50,000 and you now decide to change to £30,000 repayment and keep £20,000 as interest-only, what does it mean? Quite simply, provided you maintain your endowment policy, PEP or pension plan until maturity, you'll keep the £30,000 (and any surplus) from your investment plan!

Better still, if you change over to full repayment, you'll keep *all* the proceeds of your investment plan. That's £50,000 plus any surplus.

Does this sound too good to be true?

What's more, as you discovered in Step 1, you'll also save a staggering amount in interest charges using the repayment method. Add up the figures and you're looking at saving a king's ransom.

You may believe that by switching to a repayment mortgage you have to start again with a 25-year repayment loan. This is a common misconception and it's simply not true. You can dictate to the lender the term you want your mortgage to run, and provided you meet the lending criteria, the lender will happily lend over that period. An interest-only mortgage on the other hand is restricted by the maturity date of the investment plan – you're only paying interest on the mortgage loan until you have sufficient funds to repay the debt.

How much will it cost?

Not as much as you would imagine. It depends on interest rates, how much you want to keep of your investment plan, and how long before it matures. But in the main, very little. Here's an illustration:

Assuming your mortgage loan is £50,000 and you decide to keep £30,000 from your investment plan when it matures, your mortgage split will be £30,000 repayment and £20,000 interest-only.

Now, use the tables in Appendix B to calculate your new monthly payment. The tables are sequential in terms of the remaining years of your mortgage. If you have, say, 18 years before your investment policy matures, refer to page 120. Using the rate of interest your lender is currently charging, match the cost per £1,000 to the corresponding interest rate and multiply this figure by the number of £1,000s you require. For example, if the current interest rate is 7 per cent, the £30,000 repayment portion of your mortgage will be £249 per month (8.2844×30), plus £117 per month (5.8333×20) for the £20,000 interest-only portion of your mortgage.

The total monthly payment would be £366 compared to £292 had the full mortgage loan been all interest-only. An increase of £74 per month.

It sounds a lot; however, we're only comparing *equivalent* interest rates. Remember that your goal is to ensure you pay less than the lender's prevailing standard variable rate over the term. More about that later!

For the extra £74 per month, what effect will this have?

If interest rates were to remain at 7 per cent over the next 18 years, the additional £74 per month means that you'd repay £79,060 (£366 × 18 years × 12 months) and only hand over £20,000 from your investment policy. Total cost £99,060.

If you continued with your interest-only mortgage, however, you would have repaid £63,070 in interest and handed over £50,000 from your investment policy. Total cost £113,070.

So, not only have you kept £30,000 from your investment plan, you've also saved just over £14,000 (£113,070 – £99,060) in interest. That's a total savings value of **£44,000**.

You might argue that you've paid £15,980 (£74 × 12 months × 18 years) to save £44,000. Not true. The £15,980 is built into the total mortgage cost of £99,060; it has been *used* to save you £44,000.

Incidentally, you won't get the £14,000 interest saving in your hand. This is simply interest you would have paid extra over the term had you remained on the interest-only mortgage. The £30,000, however, is yours to keep.

Should I change over to all repayment?

The answer lies with you. If you can afford it, yes! The savings are stunning, especially if you keep your investment plan in place.

Also, bear in mind that interest rates have dropped significantly. And they're predicted to be low for a long time. Getting used to paying more for your mortgage loan shouldn't be too much of a hardship – you were paying 15.4 per cent in 1990 after all! Today's rates are around 7 per cent at the time of writing, more than 8 per cent below 1990's rate. Interestingly, in the previous example, you would pay an extra £74 on an interest-only mortgage at 8.75 per cent, just 1.75 per cent above the interest rate used.

In short, if you can afford to, now is the time to start investing your money for your future, not the lender's. However, if you can't afford to switch to full repayment, just decide how much you can afford every month and use the tables in Appendix B to 'mix and match' a part repayment, part interest-only mortgage. You'll still save an incredible sum of money.

What about making small payments when I can afford it?

If you're uncomfortable about increasing your mortgage payments, you can make additional capital payments to your lender even with an interest-only mortgage. It has the same effect since the same principle applies. Plus, it offers a degree of flexibility if your household budget is tight. But… .

First, you need discipline. You'll probably manage to keep it up for perhaps a couple of years. But in all likelihood, you'll lapse into the habit of just making your normal monthly payment. 'It's too much bother', 'Christmas was more expensive than we expected', 'the central heating needs fixing', 'we need a new washing machine…'. It happens!

Second, your lender might not let you make additional payments while you're on one of their special low interest-rate deals. Or they may charge a redemption fee to recover some the interest they'll lose. This will drastically reduce your long-term savings.

Third, if your lender operates the annual rest system, you may miss the date their accounting year ends. The lender's accounting year may not end on the last day of the calendar year. And lenders can change this date at their discretion. Misjudge this date and you'll lose a year's worth of reduced interest payments.

Lastly, you'll you have to tell the lender that your payment is to be applied to the capital part of your mortgage loan. Otherwise, it will be kept in a separate account on which they may or may not pay interest. If you forget to notify your lender what the payment is for, again, you could lose a year's worth of reduced interest payments under the annual rest system.

The best investment you'll ever make

No doubt, you're thinking there's a catch. (There isn't!) Nonetheless, being proficient on financial matters, you decide that rather than increasing your monthly mortgage payment you'll invest the extra in an investment plan. The effect would be the same, wouldn't it?

Wrong! On two counts: debt and compound interest.

Your mortgage loan is an expensive debt. And reducing your mortgage debt using the repayment method is effectively compound interest working in reverse. In other words, you're paying interest on a falling balance.

Suspecting you're still not convinced, here's an example of how reducing your debt is better than investing.

Say your interest-only mortgage loan is £50,000 with 20 years remaining. Assume the average interest rate over the 20-year term is 8.5 per cent. Your average monthly payment will be £354 and you'll repay £84,960 in interest. Plus you'll hand over £50,000 to the lender from the proceeds of your investment plan to repay the original loan. Total cost £134,960.

If you decide to switch the whole of the interest-only mortgage to the repayment method and carry on paying towards your investment plan, how much will you save?

Assuming your new lender operates the annual rest scheme for calculating interest, your average monthly payment will increase to £440, but you'll only pay £55,600 in interest. Total £105,600. So not only have you saved £29,360 in interest, you'll keep the £50,000 from your investment plan. A total savings value of **£79,360**.

However, instead of increasing your monthly payment by £86 (£440 – £354), you decide to use it to fund a reasonably safe endowment policy. Currently, £86 per month will purchase a policy that should pay out around £40,000 over 20 years. Now let's say your investment performs remarkably well and pays out almost double what you expected, an incredible £79,360!

'There! Told you so... I've gained the same, haven't I?'

Well, actually, no you've not. You've gained precisely nothing. Why? Because, although you made £79,360 from your investment, you *wasted* £79,360 paying too much for your mortgage. Net gain: £0. Ouch!

What's more, since we're talking about 'safe' investments, reasonably achieving a return of £79,360 from an endowment policy will cost in the region of £180 per month over 20 years, not £86 per month. Ouch again!

If you already have a repayment mortgage

You can save a fortune on a repayment mortgage too. How? By informing your lender you want to reduce the number of years of your term! It's that simple.

And not only will you have reduced your mortgage term in one fell swoop, you'll save a massive chunk of interest into the bargain. Moreover, if you remortgage with a lender that calculates interest using the monthly rest or daily rest scheme, you'll save even more.

Obviously, how much you'll save depends on the extra you can afford to pay every month. But even just a little extra can be a lucrative investment. Here's an example:

Let's assume your current mortgage is £50,000 with 20 years remaining. Let's also assume that the average interest rate over this term is 8.5 per cent and your lender operates the annual rest scheme for calculating interest. In this case, your average monthly payment will be £440 and you'll pay £105,600 over the 20-year term. In other words, you'll pay £55,600 in interest. Let's use this as the benchmark to see what savings can be achieved by reducing the term.

So, say you now decide to remortgage and reduce the term to 15 years. Assuming the interest rate remains the same, your new monthly mortgage payment will be £502 (an increase of just £62).

You'll now pay £90,360 to the lender over the 15 years, saving **£15,240** in interest.

You might argue that you've paid £11,160 (£62 × 12 months × 15 years) to save £15,240 in interest. Not true. The £11,160 is built into the total repayment cost of the £90,360; it has been *used* to save you £15,240 in interest *and* reduce the term.

Of course, you now have five years without making a mortgage payment. Its value, since we're comparing like for like, is **£26,400** (£440 × 12 months × 5 years).

So for an outlay of £62 per month you'll save £15,240 in interest, plus you won't pay £26,400 in mortgage payments. That's a total of **£41,640** and a profit of **373 per cent with no risk**. Can any financial adviser guarantee that? No way!

Now, if you receive just 7 per cent per annum in interest on the five years' mortgage payments you didn't have to pay to the lender, you'll receive another **£4,580**.

That's a total of **£46,220** by simply paying £62 extra a month on your mortgage for 15 years, and investing the remaining five years' payments at a rate below the mortgage interest rate. That's a profit of **414 per cent** on your £11,160 investment with no risk.

Can you afford not to do it?

Remortgage to save even more

In each of the examples so far, the monthly mortgage payment has increased to achieve the savings. This is because we have only considered comparing like for like in terms of interest rates. Taking the example used at the very beginning of this chapter, you'll agree that maintaining a lower interest rate over the term is both prudent and effective. Clearly, reducing your monthly mortgage payment means paying less interest. And that means remortgaging, either with your current lender or with a new lender.

Step 3 shows you how to remortgage safely and successfully. The main pitfall of remortgaging, as you'll discover, is redemption penalties. However, provided you avoid paying redemption penalties each time you remortgage, you'll gain (in most instances). Which means that you may have to accept being tied to the lender's prevailing variable interest rate for a couple of years after, say, a three-year fixed rate. Accept it. Lowering your *average* interest rate over the term is the key to saving money.

To illustrate the savings you can achieve on your monthly payments and the overall saving on the total cost of your mortgage, here's another example:

As the benchmark, assume your interest-only mortgage loan is £50,000 with 20 years remaining, and the assumed average interest rate over this term is 8.5 per cent.

If you have an interest-only mortgage, your monthly payment will be £354 and you'll pay £84,960 in interest. Plus you'll hand over £50,000 from your investment plan. Total cost £134,960.

If you decide to split your mortgage £30,000 repayment, £20,000 interest-only, your monthly payment will be £406 and you'll pay £97,440 in interest, plus you'll hand over £20,000 from your investment plan. Total cost £117,440 but you keep £30,000. Total savings value: £47,520.

And if you decide to convert your mortgage to full repayment, your monthly payment will be £440 and you'll pay £55,600 in interest. Total cost £105,600 but you keep £50,000. Total savings value: £79,360.

How much would you save by remortgaging to a lower interest rate?

Let's say that you remortgage every five years over the 20-year term. You secure a 3.2 per cent discount for two years in each remortgaged period. The tie-in period each time you remortgage is five years, which means that for three years out of five you are at 8.5 per cent. However, your *average* interest rate will have dropped to 7.25 per cent over the 20-year term.

How do the figures compare with a mortgage that's split £30,000 repayment, £20,000 interest-only? Your new mortgage payment on average would be £362 per month compared to £406, a saving of £44 per month. The lower interest rate would have resulted in a total of £106,880 paid to the lender compared to £117,440, a saving of

£10,560. More importantly, the total savings value over the full interest-only mortgage is **£58,080** for just **£8** more a month.

If you decide to change to full repayment, your new mortgage payment on average would be £401 per month compared to £440, a saving of £39 per month. The lower interest rate would result in a total of £96,240 paid to the lender compared to £105,600, a saving of £9,360.

The total savings value over the full interest-only mortgage is **£88,720** for just **£47** more a month.

Impressed?

In addition, the third step to unlocking a few more thousands is to remortgage with a lender operating a monthly rest or daily rest scheme (see Appendix A); you'll also reduce the amount of interest you'll be charged over the term. If you choose to remortgage with a lender who charges interest using the monthly rest scheme, in the previous examples, you'll save an additional £960 on the split repayment and interest-only mortgage, and £1,440 in interest on the full repayment mortgage at no extra cost to yourself. Totals: **£59,040** and **£90,160** respectively.

Inspired?

Surrender or save?

If you'd like to switch over completely to a repayment mortgage, but the monthly mortgage payment including your investment plan is beyond your reach, what are your options?

If you're using an endowment policy to repay your mortgage loan at the end of the term, consider selling or surrendering it. (Remember that you'll need term life assurance to cover your mortgage loan should you die over the term.) Not only will this free up some money in the short term, you'll probably save on your total monthly outgoings too. However, if you *maintain* your current monthly outgoings, you'll probably be able to reduce the number of years remaining on your mortgage loan too.

For example, say your interest-only mortgage loan is £50,000 with 20 years remaining, and your endowment policy costs £98 per month. Assume the average interest rate over the remaining 20-year term will be 8.5 per cent. Your average monthly payment will be £354 and you'll repay £84,960 in interest plus you'll hand over £50,000 to the lender from the proceeds of your endowment policy. Total cost £134,960.

You want to change to repayment but can't afford to increase your monthly mortgage expenditure. So, you surrender your endowment policy and remortgage to a full repayment mortgage with a lender operating the annual rest scheme.

Applying the same mortgage *outgoings* of £452 per month (£354 + £98) on a repayment mortgage at the same interest rate, you'll repay £97,630 to the lender, saving **£37,330** in interest. Plus you'll repay the mortgage loan after 18 years. That means a total of **£10,850** in monthly payments you won't need to make. Total savings value: **£48,180**.

Now, you won't get much back from your endowment policy if you surrender it – maybe around £5,000 even although you've contributed £5,880. So you may have lost £880 from the endowment, but you've gained £48,180 by changing to repayment over the long term and gained £5,000 in the short term. Of course, if you put the £5,000 into an ISA, for instance, and leave it for the 20 years, assuming 9 per cent growth per annum will net you £21,420 (and that's including a 5 per cent initial charge plus an annual charge of 0.75 per cent). That's a total savings value of **£69,600**.

Consolidating debt

Credit cards and charge cards are expensive. With an APR of typically 20 per cent (and even more with charge cards) you'll pay a small fortune in interest if you only pay the minimum required every month.

Provided you have the equity, there's nothing to stop you getting rid of this debt by consolidating it within your mortgage loan. That way, you'll be paying the lender's interest rate, which is far less than the credit card companies, although you'll be paying the debt for longer.

The question is, should you wait until you clear your credit card debt before reducing your mortgage debt, or is it better to consolidate?

The average credit card debt in the UK at the time of writing is around £2,000. (Does that make you feel better or worse?) The minimum monthly payment for credit cards is usually 5 per cent of the balance. For £2,000 debt, this is £100 per month. Getting rid of that and using the £100 instead towards reducing your mortgage debt is rather tempting, isn't it? Not only would you be getting rid of expensive interest charges, you'd be *investing* your money for *you*, not the credit card company.

How long would it take to clear a £2,000 credit card debt if you paid £100 a month until the debt was clear? Two years.

However, if you added the debt onto your interest-only mortgage of, say, £50,000 and switched to repayment, how much would you save compared to waiting for two years before switching?

If you decide to clear the credit card debt first, you'd repay £2,400 to the credit card company. Now, assuming a 20-year mortgage term at an average interest rate over this term of 7 per cent, you'll repay £7,000 in interest over the two years on the interest-only mortgage, and £39,420 in interest over the remaining 18 years on the repayment mortgage. Total cost £48,820.

Switching your mortgage to full repayment with the credit card debt included (with the same average interest rate over the 20-year term) results in £48,160 paid in interest.

Which means you'd save £660 by consolidating your debt, rather than waiting before changing to the repayment mortgage. Of course, if you maintain a lower interest rate than the 7 per cent used in this example you'll save even more.

Will lenders always allow you to consolidate debt? That depends how much you want to consolidate. In general you can increase your mortgage loan up to 95 per cent of the value of your property (although you may incur a MIP fee – see Step 3) if you want to consolidate debt or raise capital.

Like to retire early with an additional lump sum?

If your goal is to retire early, the last thing you need is monthly mortgage payments eating into your retirement fund. If your mortgage is finally repaid when you reach 65, but you want to retire at 60, switching to repayment is the only answer.

Using the techniques already described will ensure you pay as little as possible in interest charges, and, if you have an investment plan, you'll get to keep all the proceeds plus any surplus.

Can you afford an extra £100 per month?

With interest rates looking likely to remain low for a long spell, imagine you could spare £100 per month to reduce your mortgage debt.

If you use all three techniques (low interest rate, switch to repayment, use lender operating the monthly or daily rest scheme), your £100 a month will reward you with huge savings. For example:

Assume your current interest-only mortgage is £50,000 and you have 18 years remaining before your investment plan matures. Assume that the average interest rate over this term will be 8 per cent. Your monthly payment would be £333 and you'll pay £71,920 in interest. Plus, you'll hand over the £50,000 from your investment plan. Total cost £121,920.

Switching your mortgage to all repayment, maintaining an average interest rate 2.25 per cent below over the term, and using a lender who calculates interest using the monthly rest scheme will save you £49,000 in interest. Plus, you'll repay your mortgage loan four years early. The value of four years' mortgage payments at £333 per month is £15,980 and if it's invested at 5 per cent per annum, its value will be £18,000. And, of course, you'll pocket £50,000 plus any surplus from your investment policy. Total savings value? **£117,000,** all for £100 a month extra for 14 years. Unbelievable, isn't it?

Don't bite off more than you can chew

You've probably looked at these figures in disbelief. No wonder! The sums involved are huge. And a mortgage loan of just £50,000 has been used in all the examples. If your mortgage loan is more than £50,000 you stand to save even more. In fact, you wouldn't believe how much you can save on a £100,000 mortgage loan!

Naturally, how much you increase your mortgage payments to reduce your mortgage debt has to be balanced with your household budget. Your circumstances may change at any time, making unforeseen demands on your funds tomorrow or in the future. So, although reducing your debt should remain one of your main priorities as part of your long-term investment plan, don't forget about having spare cash available for tomorrow's emergencies.

If you have an investment plan in place now, keep it going. It may not be the most adventurous investment, but it is reasonably safe. Only convert to repayment what you can afford a month. You can always increase the mortgage split more in your favour when you remortgage again. Put simply, don't extend yourself beyond your means if you want your home to remain so.

STEP 3

Better the devil you know?

How remortgaging can save you thousands in the short term, how to go about it, and how to avoid the pitfalls

Quite frankly, there's never a good time or a bad time to remortgage. Interest rates are a moving target, and predicting long-term shifts is impossible. Having said that, mortgage interest rates are at an unprecedented low and that trend looks likely to continue in the short to medium term. Consequently, there are many extremely attractive deals in the marketplace as lenders vie for increased business.

But a word to the wise: there are pitfalls for the unwary. Hence the reason for this chapter – to help you assess what's on offer and understand the potential hazards so that you make an informed choice. You'll find out how the various mortgage products work, and how the different flavours of 'mortgage' available stack up against traditional loans. Plus, you'll uncover a few more tricks the lenders have up their sleeves to help you part company with your cash.

This chapter reveals all!

Why you should take advantage of low interest rates

If you are one of the estimated 7 million currently paying the highest interest on your mortgage, you won't be surprised to learn that you are subsidizing the other 5 million that aren't.

In short, if you're not on a low interest rate, you're on the lender's standard variable rate (SVR). And it's the most expensive rate to be on. Remortgaging to a lower interest rate inevitably results in monthly mortgage savings. This can be used to offset the increase in your monthly mortgage payments when switching to full repayment, or part repayment, part interest-only, or if you intend reducing the term of your repayment mortgage.

You might have already been on a low rate and are now locked into the lender's SVR for a few years. Nonetheless, it could still be your advantage to pay the penalty to secure a more favourable rate. Especially now that you know that maintaining a rate below the lender's SVR eliminates costly interest charges over the longer term. This, however, requires you to do some sums.

What are the benefits?

Remortgaging offers five irresistible benefits and is, in most cases, fundamental to achieving the remarkable savings shown in Step 2.

First, you can change the parameters of your mortgage as outlined in the previous chapter. This guarantees that you'll be reducing the mortgage capital even during the low-interest period – unlike making lump sum payments every once in a while.

Second, you could reduce your monthly outgoings overnight and possibly save thousands of pounds in the short term. Alternatively, you may want to use part of the monthly savings to increase the repayment part of your mortgage. You'll have to be confident your income will rise during the low-interest term to accommodate for your return to SVR.

Third, you can get rid of 'bad' debt, for example, by consolidating high-interest credit card or charge card debt. If you have the equity, this is virtually essential.

Fourth, you can free up part of the equity in your home to fund perhaps a once-in-a-lifetime holiday at very low cost.

And lastly, you can remortgage every three to five years depending on your lock-in period. The net result is that the interest rate over the remaining term of your mortgage will average less than SVR. And that means big savings.

And the downside?

Naturally, there are some drawbacks too. For example, it's likely that you'll be locked in to the lender's SVR for a number of years after your low interest-rate deal ends. Redeeming your mortgage (that is, getting out of the deal) during this period can prove expensive.

Also, you may have to pay an arrangement fee to set up the mortgage, a valuation fee and legal fees. Plus, depending on the value of your property relative to the amount you want to borrow, you may have to pay a one-off insurance premium (an MIP) on behalf of the lender. This is used to cover *its* costs should it have to repossess and subsequently sell your home.

Not all lenders require that you make these payments. Remortgaging with your current lender, for instance, may be the most cost-effective route to securing the best deal. But even if you are forced to pay, remortgaging is almost certainly to your benefit in the short term and absolutely to your benefit in the long term.

Thankfully, remortgaging is not as traumatic as moving home. But it does take what seems like an inordinate length of time. Waiting six to eight weeks before you see your new mortgage up and running is not uncommon with a new lender – during which interest rates could fall with better deals on offer. But you have to jump at some point. If your mortgage application is straightforward, however, it could be processed within four to six weeks.

What about the paperwork?

Remortgaging is one of the highest-paid activities available today. The fruits of a few hours' effort are a saving of tens of thousands of pounds. What occupation pays an equivalent hourly rate?

If you're organized, remortgaging is easy. Later in this chapter, you'll find out exactly what you need in the way of documents, and what you'll need to know to fill in the paperwork. Although it's a chore, just think of the savings you'll make and what you have to look forward to.

If you don't want to do the paperwork yourself, you can get someone else to do it for you, either via the telephone or through a mortgage intermediary.

The difference a percentage point makes

Irrespective of what deal you ultimately secure, it's worth proving that even with redemption penalties a low interest rate is to your benefit rather than the lender's – in most cases, that is. If you have, say, a year to run before your lock-in period ends, it makes sense to hold off from remortgaging to avoid the redemption charges.

Let's do a quick calculation:

Assume that you have an interest-only mortgage of £60,000 and the redemption penalty is £2,100 at 7 per cent. Suppose you remortgage and secure a low-interest product that gives an average of 6 per cent over a five-year lock-in period.

£60,000 × 7% × 5 years = £21,000
£62,100 × 6% × 5 years = £18,630

The difference is a saving of £2,370 even with the added cost of the redemption penalty. In effect, it's a free loan for five years.

Your first port of call

Before you rush off to the lender with the lowest interest rates, your first port of call must be to your current lender. This is the path of least resistance and may eliminate some of the charges and fees outlined above. There may be some fees, but it's unlikely you'll have to pay for a valuation or stump up for legal fees.

Chances are, though, that your current lender will not be too keen to offer you its most appealing products. These are normally reserved for new business (that's loyalty for you!). Expect an offer of perhaps 0.5 per cent reduction in your current interest rate. Don't accept it. If you can't secure one of your lender's best deals, take your business elsewhere. Let's face it, all lenders need borrowers.

How do you choose?

With hundreds of lenders in the marketplace, and hundreds more products available, choosing the right low-interest-rate product looks, on the face of it, rather bewildering. Don't be daunted. This chapter will focus on your specific requirements to help narrow the field and enable you to get the most suitable and cost-effective deal for yourself.

Your financial position

Before you look at any of the low-interest products on offer, you'll need to review your current financial circumstances. This will determine what deals are available to you. If you're 'prime' (that is, you've never missed a mortgage payment or personal loan payment, you've plenty of equity in your home, good salary prospects and so on), lenders will fight for your business and you'll have access to the best rates.

At the other extreme, you may be 'sub-prime'. This refers to your credit history; you may have missed the odd mortgage payment, or had a county court judgement (CCJ) against you. The amount of time that has elapsed since you cleared your debt will determine what products you have access to.

Budgeting and assessing risk

At the same time, you'll have to examine your current outgoings and your attitude to risk. Locking yourself into a long-term fixed rate means you'll know for certain what you'll be paying over the low-interest period. This is ideal for budgeting; but there's an associated risk. If interest rates drop below the fixed level, you'll be paying more than you need to. And getting out of the deal can be costly.

Of course, nobody has a crystal ball as to what future interest rates will be. But it is possible to take an objective look at whether interest rates will rise or fall during the period of your deal.

Take, for instance, returns quoted for endowment policies. These are now quoted between 4 and 8 per cent, compared to 7.5 and 12.5 per cent not so long ago. Why? Because the Personal Investments Authority (PIA) is now very sensitive to accusations of mis-selling (remember pensions?). Life assurance companies are now required to be realistic with quoted returns on endowment policies relative to the future economic climate. This is a clear indication of how the financial services industry perceives future economic growth.

Additionally, the government has handed over the reins to the Bank of England to set interest rates. Apart from sidestepping any blame should interest rates cause problems in the economy, the government retains the right to apply pressure on the Bank of England when it suits it. This is good news since the government is intent on joining the European single currency in 2002. When this happens, the European Bank rather than the Bank of England will set interest rates. With mortgage interest rates in Europe at around 5 per cent (at the time of writing), it's understandable that the government will be anxious to gradually reduce interest rates (that is, apply pressure accordingly) to avoid potential economic catastrophes at that time. This is to everyone's advantage – with the exception of savers!

So, with interest rates predicted to be low in the short to medium term, your next task is deciding on the type of deal most suited to you. This requires some understanding of how the products work and the pros and cons of each. Before that though… .

Do you need an adviser?

The short answer is 'no'. Unless you want to be sold another expensive endowment policy or term life assurance!

Anyone giving mortgage advice, whether an independent financial adviser, tied-financial adviser, mortgage broker or intermediary, will usually want to be paid to remortgage you. Which is fair since the adviser is doing all the legwork. However, you'll be picking up the bill somewhere along the way, either in upfront fees, commission, or worse, extra and unnecessary life insurance.

You don't need to pay anything unless an hour of your time is worth more than, say, £250. Anyway, you've already paid for mortgage advice (you bought this book, didn't you?) so why fork out more? There is no substitute for taking charge of your own financial affairs.

If you must approach a mortgage adviser, reading the remainder of this chapter will, at the very least, arm you with sufficient knowledge to look beyond the packages he or she offers. On the plus side, many of the smaller lenders offer some of the best deals through intermediaries, but you'll need to make an informed judgement as to whether the content is suitable for you. Moreover, if your credit history is chequered, an adviser could be the most convenient route to sorting out the wheat from the chaff.

Fortunately, not all mortgage advisers charge. They may well receive their commission directly from the lender. But it is in your interest to establish how they receive their commission before reviewing deals.

You already have an adviser?

If you currently have a financial adviser and he or she hasn't discussed ways of saving you money on mortgage interest, consider inviting your adviser round to your home. When he or she arrives, ask why you haven't been told about this 'investment' earlier. Then embarrass your adviser by producing this book!

It sounds harsh, but why would you let anyone in the financial services industry who is supposedly looking after your finances continue to do so when he or she has overlooked such an obvious and safe method of saving you large sums of money? Or perhaps has sold you under-performing endowment policies that do nothing more than line the adviser's pockets at your expense?

Of course, good financial advisers are worth their weight in gold (perhaps not a good analogy with the recent slump in gold prices!). Many financial advisers don't touch mortgages. Even if they do, they don't necessarily give bad advice. The problem is you don't know beforehand whether their advice is good or bad – until it's too late. The fact remains, though, that financial advisers are sales-people with the goal of making money for themselves first and you second. You've been warned!

Types of product in the market

Variable (or 'floating') rate

If you're not already on a low-interest-rate product, this is what you're on. It's also known as standard variable rate (SVR) and the UK is one of the few countries that charges interest on mortgages using this method.

How SVR works is quite simple. When the lender changes its base lending rate in response to, say, the economic climate, you receive a letter shortly afterwards advising you of the change and what your new monthly mortgage payment will be. Lenders usually fall in line with interest rate changes made by the Bank of England. However, lenders have been known to delay changing their base lending rates by as much as a month when the Bank of England's base rate is cut. The result? A fortune in profit for every lender that operates the lag system.

The main disadvantage of being on SVR, apart from paying maximum interest, is that your monthly payments can go up or down without limit as the lender's base lending rate changes. This makes it hard to budget for.

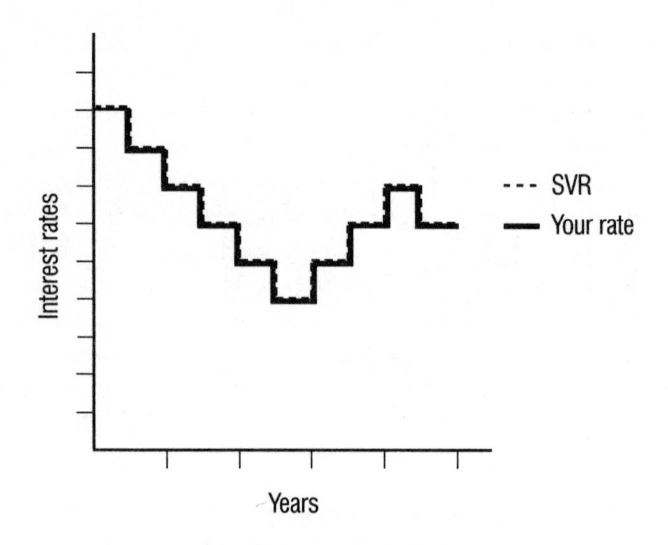

Figure 3.1 *How SVR works*

Not all lenders have the same SVR; banks and de-mutualized building societies tend to have a slightly higher SVR (they have to satisfy their shareholders, after all) than mutual building societies.

One advantage of being on SVR is that you can usually make additional payments to reduce your loan without penalty. But, even then, some lenders make this difficult, insisting on a minimum payment equal to six months' mortgage payments. And depending on how the lender calculates interest on your loan (that is, annual, monthly or daily rest – see Appendix A), you may not see the benefit of your extra payments until the beginning of the lender's new accounting year.

Discounted rate

Discounted rates operate in exactly the same way as SVR, and they are often confused with one another. The difference, though, is that you are guaranteed to be below SVR at the level of discount set by the lender. In other words, your discounted rate tracks the lender's standard variable rate, maintaining the same differential during the discounted term.

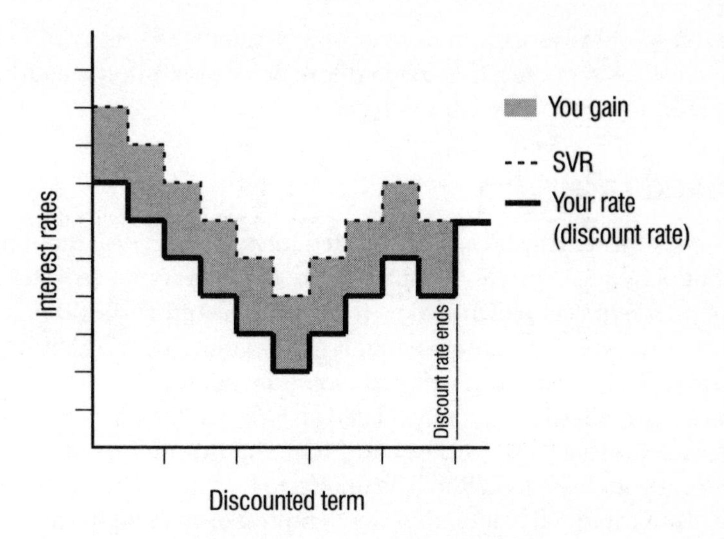

Figure 3.2 *How discounts work*

The main feature of a discounted rate is that you are guaranteed to save money throughout the discounted term. In short, there's no risk element attached to it. If you're borrowing well within your means, this is the deal to go for.

On the other hand, if your budget is strained by varying levels of rate change, this is probably not the best product to choose. But even if this is the case, don't dismiss a discounted rate out of hand. The reason is that you've probably experienced rate changes in the past and will undoubtedly do so in the future. Building a degree of flexibility into your budget to accommodate fluctuations is good practice. That's because you're unlikely to stretch your mortgage debt beyond what you think you can reasonably pay back each month.

With a discounted rate, should interest rates rise substantially during the discounted term, you may not save as much as with, say, a fixed rate product. Conversely, if interest rates drop substantially you will still gain, whereas the savings from a fixed rate product are reduced, or worse, wiped out.

In summary, provided you have a budget that can cope with varying payments, this is one of the best low-rate products on offer since you always gain, whatever your lender's SVR is. And with interest rates predicted to remain low or even fall in the short to medium term, you have most to gain.

Fixed rate

Fixed rates are riskier than discounted rates, but are ideal for budgeting. Fixed rate products usually have the lowest interest rates in the marketplace, which makes them very tempting. But dangers lurk. If you're unfortunate enough to see your lender's SVR drop below your fixed rate threshold, you'll be stranded paying more back in interest than if you had been on SVR. On the flip side, you'll have the satisfaction of knowing that should interest rates rise during your fixed term you'll be unaffected.

On a cautionary note, don't be tempted into a long-term fixed rate if you can help it. Five years is a reasonable maximum. Long-term fixed rates are always higher than short-term rates, and outmanoeuvring the money markets is not what fixed rates are about. Use a fixed rate strictly for budgeting.

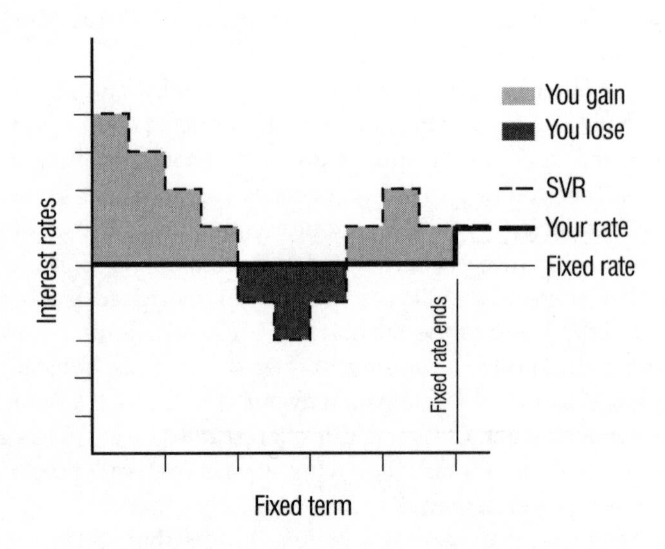

Figure 3.3 *How fixed rates work*

In summary, a fixed rate offers complete certainty in your monthly outgoings during the fixed term. And provided you secure a fixed rate that's well below SVR, both now and what's predicted in the future, you'll gain. By how much is uncertain. A fixed rate is riskier than a discounted rate, but if interest rates rise, you'll gain more – although it could be a painful jump when you return to SVR.

Capped rate

This product is a compromise between the discounted rate and fixed rate. It offers the best of both worlds and is clearly the safest option, combining reduced risk and convenient budgeting.

The cap is simply a ceiling – it's the maximum interest rate you'll be charged while the cap is in force. Your monthly payments won't rise above the cap when interest rates go up; however, if the lender's SVR drops below the ceiling, your monthly payments drop to the same level. Unlike a discount rate, you don't gain if this happens since you're back on SVR. But you don't lose either if you opted for a fixed rate.

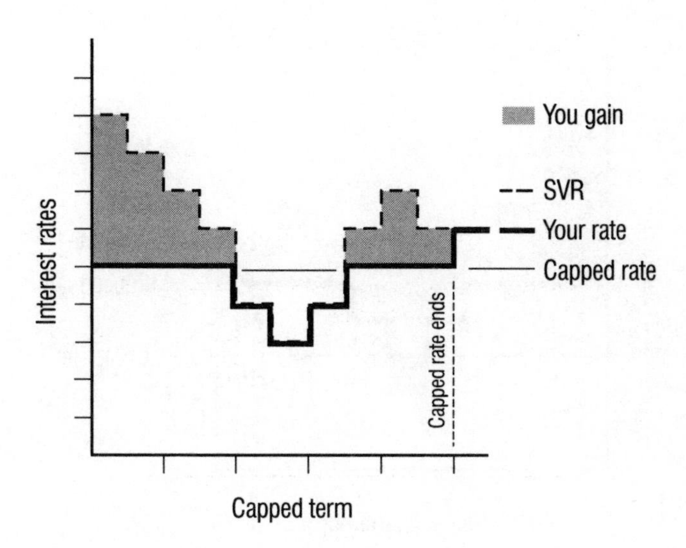

Figure 3.4 *How capped rates work*

Most capped rates are well below the lender's SVR, but are usually set slightly higher than fixed rate levels. Long-term capped rates are the norm. This makes for easier budgeting since you'll know exactly what you'll be paying over the capped term. And you have the potential to benefit if the lender's SVR falls below the cap.

A variation on the capped rate is the 'cap and collar'. The 'collar' is the floor, and it's the minimum interest rate you'll be charged while the collar is in force. If the lender's SVR drops below the collar, your monthly payments are held at the collar threshold; in effect, you'll be paying more than SVR. 'Cap and collar' deals are not very common today, but they may come back as lenders attempt to cover their costs with falling interest rates.

In summary, a capped rate offers the certainty of a fixed rate without the risk of being stranded at a higher rate should interest rates fall below the cap. You don't gain over SVR should interest rates drop below the cap, but neither do you lose. If there is uncertainty as to whether interest rates will rise or fall, you can bet 'each way' by securing a capped rate.

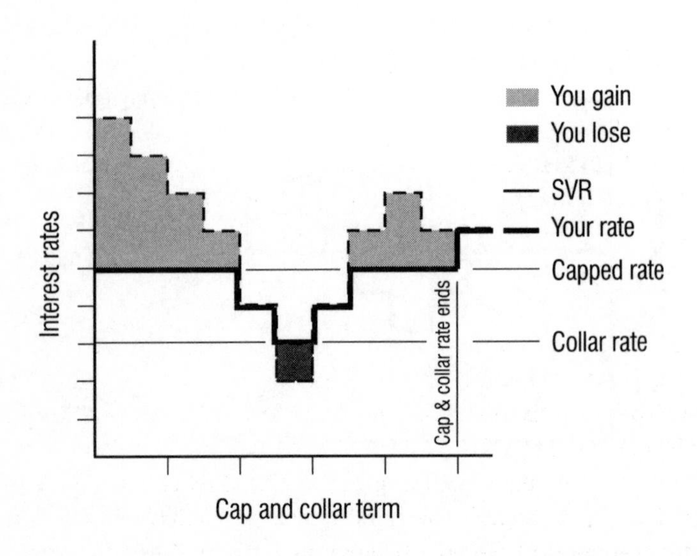

Figure 3.5 *How 'cap and collar' rates work*

Cash-backs

Cash-back products are ideal if you are in need of ready cash or need a deposit to buy a property. But you don't get something for nothing. The lender wants your continued business for a pre-determined term. Otherwise it will expect part, if not all, of the cash returned. So, while you make an instant gain, you'll be typically on the lender's highest rate (SVR) for the lock-in period.

You will of course have made a guaranteed 'saving' which in itself is bankable. This isn't assured with a fixed or capped rate. You could even invest the money and hope for a higher rate of return compared to what you might have saved with one of the above products. But you'll have to work your investment hard.

Some cash-backs are quite generous, usually a percentage (around 5 per cent) of the amount borrowed up to a pre-set maximum, and are paid on completion of the mortgage. There are variations too; you might secure part cash-back plus a discount; or secure part cash-back, part fixed rate. Obviously, lenders won't offer you a large cash-back sum or the best discount or fixed rate, as they have to recoup their costs somehow. But it's entirely up to you how you spend the money, and the cash-back could be used to meet some of the fees when remortgaging.

In summary, cash-backs aren't suitable if you're on a tight budget, although ready cash may be desirable in some instances. Furthermore, you're likely to save more by choosing another type of product, both monthly and over the product's term.

Cocktails

Some lenders allow you to construct your own type of loan from the various products described. For example, you can split your loan, with 50 per cent fixed and 50 per cent at SVR. Or 70 per cent capped and 30 per cent at SVR.

There are two benefits to doing this. The first is that you spread the risk if you're unsure whether interest rates will rise or fall during your lock-in period. Second, by keeping part on SVR, you can make additional lump sum payments to this portion without incurring redemption penalties. This can be particularly useful if your salary includes bonuses.

You're not restricted to just two splits, either. Some lenders allow you up to five different split combinations with, say, four tiered fixed rates and a portion on SVR. Discount rates, though, are generally restricted to just one portion.

Mortgages with pitfalls

To set the record straight, there's no such animal as an 'annual review', 'flexible', 'bi-weekly' or 'euro' mortgage. They are merely references to the method of making your monthly mortgage payment. For example, a flexible mortgage usually allows you to overpay (make additional payments) or underpay without incurring charges.

In all cases, you still use the traditional repayment mortgage method or interest-only method to repay the mortgage loan. So don't be fooled by clever marketing, because as you're about to find out, these methods are full of quirks and flaws.

Annual review

If you are on the lender's SVR, you may also be on an annual review scheme. This scheme allows you to maintain your monthly mortgage payment at the same level throughout the year. At the beginning of the following year, the lender adjusts the interest rate you'll be charged by calculating the rolled-up interest of the previous year.

Although this scheme provides a year of certainty as to your monthly outgoings, you run the risk of a dramatic jump in monthly payments if interest rates have risen over the previous year.

They're also expensive to escape from if you decide to change lenders. The redemption penalty is usually all the interest owed to the end of the lending year. If you decide to switch lenders and are on this scheme, wait until at least a few months before the year ends.

Flexible mortgages

Lenders jockeying for market share are always on the lookout for new ideas to attract new business. The latest is 'flexible' mortgages, and they're becoming increasingly popular as advertising hits its mark.

But be careful of the marketing hype. Flexible mortgages are really only beneficial if you have an irregular income – for example if you're self-employed, work on fixed contracts, a company director, or if your salary is made up with bonuses at the end of the year. Why? Because if your income is erratic, you can make underpayments when necessary – *provided* you've also made overpayments.

If you're in steady employment, they're not such a good deal. The first reason is that the interest rates are often higher than those offered on the High Street. The mortgage providers usually have them slightly below SVR to encourage you through their doors, but the rates don't last for very long before you're back paying their highest interest rate.

Secondly, you may be expected to set up your current account with the lender. This may seem like a good idea, but question why. If you set up all your direct debits and standing orders with the lender, are you likely to go through the whole rigmarole again six months later when your initial low rate reverts to its SVR? Look beyond the glossy packaging. The lender is relying on your being averse to going through the whole process again with another lender. And you'll be caught.

Third, many of these deals require that you increase your monthly payment year on year to make the projected savings. It's usually in the region of 3 per cent. Now, if your monthly payment is £300, you'll pay an additional £9 the following year. It's not much. If that's all you pay, not only will you have little equity in your home for many years, by the 15th year, you'll be paying more than £450 a month. Which means you could still be paying a large chunk of your salary each month to repay your mortgage. Whereas, the more you can pay now to reduce your mortgage debt, the faster your equity will grow. And you won't have added pressure applied to your future monthly outgoings.

Fourth, you can take payment holidays. Sounds attractive, doesn't it? But, if you're serious about reducing your mortgage debt, this simply negates all the effort you made reducing the mortgage debt in the first place. Each payment you miss, the more your debt will increase.

Current account mortgages

Another variation on how you pay your mortgage loan is to consolidate all your loans and savings into one account: a mortgage current account. This mortgage product recently arrived here from Australia, where around a third of new home loans are of this type.

The idea is that when your salary is paid into the account, your mortgage debt is reduced. And because interest on your debt is calculated daily, less interest is charged compared to a traditional mortgage account. As funds are drawn from the account to pay bills and living expenses, however, the interest charged increases. Although the interest saving is slight every month, the cumulative effect – in theory – should save thousands of pounds over the term. By how much depends on how well the account is managed.

It's a good idea but with flaws: you're supplied with a cheque book and a switch/debit card and it allows for standing orders and direct debits. If you make an unauthorized overdraft, you're penalized very heavily.

Also, interest rates offered with this type of product aren't as competitive as those found on the High Street. (And you know how much difference a few percentage points can make to the overall cost of the mortgage!) And, while their interest rates may look attractive given that you can also borrow money to repay personal loan and credit card debt, there's nothing to stop you consolidating these debts into a traditional mortgage – at a significantly reduced interest rate.

In addition, the best interest rates are available only to those with around 50 per cent equity, or those earning six-figure salaries. And even then, the interest rates available are typically only 1 per cent below most High Street lenders' SVR.

Bi-weekly mortgages

These are also known as 'accelerator' mortgages. Again, the naming convention refers to the way you make payments to the lender rather than its being a new type of mortgage. These mortgages are currently marketed by a number of mortgage brokers.

So how do they work? Normally, you make 12 monthly payments (that is, calendar months) to your lender over the year. If you were to pay half your normal monthly payment on the 1st of the month and the other half on the 15th of the month, and carried on throughout the whole year paying in this way, you would have made 26 payments in total to the lender. Twenty-six fortnightly payments are the equivalent of 13 months' payments. So, in effect, you make an extra month's payment to the lender each year. This is then applied as a capital payment to reduce the amount of interest you'll pay in the following and subsequent years.

You don't have to pay fortnightly (although you can); the above is merely an illustration of how the system works. If you were to pay monthly, the 13th payment is divided by 12 months and simply added to your normal monthly payment. For example, if your current monthly payment were £300, you'd make monthly payments of £325 (£300 × 13 ÷ 12) to accrue the 13th payment.

How does this affect your savings? In exactly the same way as shown in Step 2 since the same principles are applied. However, there are a number of drawbacks.

To begin with, the broker has to set up a savings (feeder) account on your behalf. From this account your lender receives your current monthly payment while the little extra you contribute accumulates. When the little extra has accrued to a full month's mortgage payment, it's transferred and credited to your mortgage account. Simple enough, but you pay a small amount each month for the privilege.

Then there are the broker's fees. These are very expensive and can add thousands onto your mortgage over the term. Worse still, they're not justified – most brokers negotiate commissions from lenders for putting volume business their way. Why pay the broker over and above what he or she already earns from the lender when you can achieve the same results using part repayment, part interest-only?

Furthermore, and more importantly, you're remortgaged into a low-interest-rate product. This means that your 13th payment may be in breach of the lender's conditions for early repayment. Consequently, the 13th payment may not have any effect until you return to SVR, or you will pay a part-redemption fee to the lender. In contrast, using the techniques in Step 2, you reduce your mortgage debt immediately, even on a low interest rate, with maximum impact.

Euro mortgages

Rather like foreign currency mortgages that became fashionable in the mid-1990s, euro mortgages will probably suffer the same fate: brevity. Why? Because it's currency speculation at the sharp end, and if you don't 'speculate' well, you could end up paying more for your mortgage even though you borrowed at a lower interest rate. In any case, unless you are paid in euros, lenders won't offer you a euro mortgage.

If you are paid in euros, here's the dilemma: If your mortgage is in sterling and the pound rises against the euro, your euro income might not convert to enough pounds to cover the cost of your monthly payments. Whereas, if your mortgage is in euros and the pound falls against the euro, your debt will rise in sterling terms while your house price remains the same – effectively reducing your equity. Selling your home at this time could lose you whatever equity has built up. Naturally, the converse of these scenarios is true and you could gain.

If you have the option to be paid in euros, think carefully before taking a euro mortgage. Unless you like monitoring currency movements and making predictions, avoid euro and other foreign currency loans. Stick with a low-interest product in sterling, it's safer!

100 per cent mortgages

If you don't have a deposit to put down on a property, you can take a 100 per cent mortgage. This is a loan that covers the full value of the property (the survey value) – but not what you pay for it. If you need to borrow more than the full value of the property, some lenders will offer up to 125 per cent.

These mortgages are expensive since you have no equity. Not only will you pay slightly above the lender's SVR, you could be charged an expensive indemnity insurance premium (MIP). This is the lender's way of covering its risk should you fail to keep up repayments and it has to repossess and sell your home. The insurance premium is paid by you and can be added to your mortgage loan.

While a 100 per cent mortgage may get you on the first rung of the property ladder, you'll pay excessively for the loan. The better option is to take a mortgage with a large cash-back component and use this as your deposit. This type of deal also means you're on the lender's SVR, not higher.

How much will it cost?

Unfortunately, remortgaging isn't expense-free. On the other hand, you can consolidate all the fees and charges onto your new mortgage provided you have the equity.

The costs associated with remortgaging can be divided into two categories: fees to the new lender, and charges by your current lender. Apart from redemption penalties, the overall cost to your mortgage debt is relatively minor.

Typically, fees to the new lender include an arrangement or booking fee, an administration fee, legal fees, a valuation fee and possibly an MIP. Part of the arrangement fee might include a reservation fee (to reserve the funds) and is not refundable should you decide not to proceed with the deal.

Charges by your current lender include redemption (even if you're on SVR), a sealing fee, and a deeds dispatch fee.

Also, check out your current mortgage statement. Your current mortgage may have the original arrangement fee and, possibly, an MIP added to it. So, for example, what you thought was a £50,000 mortgage loan might in reality be £50,750.

The new lender will add (in most cases) the new arrangement fee and any MIP to your mortgage loan after it has agreed to advance you the loan. Which means you'll also pay interest on them over the mortgage term, like all the other fees you choose to consolidate in your new mortgage loan.

The value of your property

One of the most important points the lender will consider on your application to remortgage is how much equity you have. Remember that equity is the amount you owe on your mortgage loan compared to the value of your property. For remortgaging purposes, equity is termed the 'loan-to-value' (LTV) ratio and is expressed as a percentage. And it's the LTV ratio that determines what products you qualify for and whether an MIP is added.

The LTV calculation is easy (although you'll probably need a calculator!); simply divide the amount you want to borrow by the current estimated value of your home. For example, if you want to borrow £60,000 and your property is valued at £75,000, the LTV is 80 per cent (£60,000 ÷ £75,000 × 100).

The lower your LTV ratio the better your chances are of securing the lowest interest rate deals. Conversely, the higher your LTV ratio (usually above 75 per cent), the more limited the product options are and they are usually at a slightly higher interest rate. Plus you could be caught with an MIP.

What are MIPs?

A mortgage indemnity policy (MIP) is a one-off payment made to the lender when your loan-to-value exceeds a certain threshold. It's also known as mortgage indemnity guarantee insurance (MIG), a higher lending fee, a higher percentage advance fee, an additional security fee, an indemnity bond, or a risk charge. Whatever term the lenders use, you don't benefit from it in any way.

The lender uses your MIP payment to purchase an insurance policy. This policy insures *the lender* should you default on your mortgage payments and it subsequently repossesses and sells your property. The insurance policy covers the lender for the difference (if any) between the full amount owed and the amount received from the sale of your property. This does not mean your debt is cleared; the insurer issuing the policy has the right to sue you for the amount it pays out to the lender for up to 12 years after the loss occurred. The argument is that you are responsible for the whole debt, not the insurance company.

MIPs generally come into effect when your loan-to-value ratio exceeds 75 per cent. More common is 85 per cent, and it's almost inevitable at 90 per cent and above. Some lenders have abolished them and instead charge a slightly higher interest rate on the same product. This can actually be even more expensive over the term.

MIP rates are also tiered. For example, between 75 and 85 per cent the MIP rate is around 4.5 per cent; between 85 and 90 per cent it's around 6 per cent; and between 90 and 95 per cent it's around 8 per cent.

Calculating an MIP

Assume that the loan you require is £50,000 and your property is valued at £55,000:

1. Calculate your loan-to-value ratio to check whether it qualifies for the lender's MIP. For example, £50,000 ÷ £55,000 × 100 = 91% (it does!).

2. Multiply your property value by the lender's minimum MIP threshold (usually 75%). In this case: £55,000 × 75% = £41,250.
3. Subtract this figure from the loan required: £50,000 – £41,250 = £8,750.
4. Multiply this figure by the MIP rate for the band into which your LTV falls. In this case: £8,750 × 8% = £700.

The £700 represents the MIP fee and will either be charged up front or added to your mortgage loan. If it's added to the mortgage loan, you'll pay interest on it for the remainder of the term. And that makes it quite expensive. The only way to reduce or avoid paying an MIP is to borrow less (if possible).

What strings are attached?

Redemption periods

The first is a redemption or 'lock-in' period linked with an early redemption penalty. Redemption periods are the lender's way of making it unattractive for you to change to another deal during your low-interest period, or attempt to repay part or your entire mortgage loan. If you try to escape the deal during this period, you'll be hit with a stiff redemption penalty.

There's much discussion about abolishing redemption periods, especially those that go beyond the reduced interest rate period. However, for the time being, they're a fact of mortgage life.

Redemption penalties vary from lender to lender. Most common is either a charge equivalent to six months' gross interest payments or 5 per cent of your mortgage loan. Typically, that means a couple of thousand pounds in charges. Others have a reducing penalty charge, where the penalty drops by one month's gross interest or 1 per cent in successive years. And then there is the incredibly vindictive market-to-market penalty. This method has a rather complicated system of calculating the charge. In essence, as interest rates drop the higher the charge – no matter how long the lock-in period is. It's not uncommon for borrowers to face charges of tens of thousands of pounds. Consequently, don't ever remortgage with a lender operating this redemption scheme.

Not all low-interest rate deals have redemption periods. This means you can switch to another lender at any time and capitalize on a lower interest rate. If you can secure a redemption-free deal that offers a similar interest rate to a deal with a lock-in period, take it. You simply can't lose.

If you are locked into a low-interest deal and you want out, some lenders offer to pay the redemption penalty for you. You'll have to do a little digging to find out who, though.

If you ever thought that lenders could lose by offering low interest-rate deals, think again! The reason is they buy the funds from the money markets at a lower rate than offered to the consumer. When the funds run out, the lender simply returns to the money markets to buy again. Whether the money markets are buoyant or depressed will determine the rate at which the lender sells the funds on.

Building and contents insurance

Another stipulation with many of the most attractive deals is that the lender will tie you into its building and contents insurance. The insurance is poor value, with premiums usually double those of mainstream insurance companies offering equivalent cover. If you don't want to take the lender's insurance, it will either increase the interest rate by perhaps 0.25 per cent or decline the deal on offer.

Lending guidelines

From the lenders' point of view, you're a risk! As such, they have to assess whether you're a good risk or a bad risk. And their lending criteria help them decide what category you fall into.

It doesn't matter that you already have a mortgage – your circumstances may have changed considerably since you took your original mortgage out. Neither does it matter that you always make your mortgage payment every month (although it helps!). Your property may have fallen in value. You may have large debts now. Or your income may have dropped. Having said that, lenders need to lend money if they're to profit. It's their *raison d'être* after all.

To this end, the lender takes each application on its current merits, assessing both your current personal status and the property on which the loan is secured. Obviously, if you're sticking with your existing lender, processing your application is much faster since your lender will already know your circumstances. Better still, you probably won't need a valuation and the lender's solicitors will prepare all the legal paperwork.

The main things a new lender will take into consideration before advancing you the loan are income, your current credit commitments, and the property, all of which are discussed below in more detail. Beyond this, you'll need to:

- ☐ state the mortgage term (lenders won't let you remortgage with under five years remaining);
- ☐ state the method of repayment (interest-only, repayment, or split);
- ☐ state whether you're a resident of the UK (it's hard to sue a non-resident in the event of mortgage loss);
- ☐ state your employer's name and address (to corroborate income and employment details);
- ☐ state your marital status and dependants (and details of maintenance payments if any);
- ☐ state proposed occupants 17 years of age or older who won't be party to the mortgage (England and Wales only);
- ☐ provide P60s of all applicants;
- ☐ provide your current mortgage statement;
- ☐ provide at least six months' bank statements for all applicants;
- ☐ provide two pieces of identification to prove you are who you say you are (for fraud prevention).

When it comes to filling in your mortgage application, make sure you have the necessary paperwork to hand – it makes life a lot less frustrating!

Income

Lenders typically base the borrowing capability on a multiple (usually three) of the gross income of the main borrower plus all secondary income. If overtime, bonuses or commission are guaranteed you can add them on; if not, the lender will use its discretion as to what can be safely added on. For sales-related occupations, the lender normally takes an average of the previous three years' income.

Many lenders exceed these multiples, for example, if your future prospects look healthy or when interest rates are low. But in general, income multiples are there to protect both the lender and the borrower and ensure monthly mortgage payments can be safely met.

Credit commitments

If you have a hire purchase agreement, a personal bank loan, or possess a credit card or charge card, the lender will need details. For two reasons: first, to determine your ability to pay the mortgage loan; and second, to assess your credit worthiness.

If you have a personal loan with, say, two years remaining at £50 a month and £2,000 on your credit card (with a minimum monthly payment of £100), the lender will deduct your yearly contribution to these debts from your gross income. This new figure is used as your gross yearly income. So, say, your gross annual salary is £17,000, the lender will deduct £600 (12 months × £50) plus £1,200 (12 months × £100), and use £15,200 (£17,000 – £1,800) as your gross yearly income.

The lender will also run a credit search to check your credit history. If you have defaulted on any payments in the previous six years or have been in arrears, it will be detected. Provided you disclose this information (and have cleared the debt!) the lender will usually use discretion and override its credit scoring system. Nondisclosure makes lenders nervous – you could be hiding something else, after all.

Your home

Since your house is used as security for the loan, the lender will need an indication of its current value. The lender normally instructs its own valuer to carry out the valuation.

The valuer will confirm the type of property, including method of construction, whether there are proposed alterations, the tenure of property (freehold, leasehold including years unexpired, feudal), and whether your estimated value is in line with similar properties in the area.

The latter point is obviously subjective. If the valuer considers your property to be worth less than your estimated value, and your loan-to-value ratio is tight, you may incur an MIP. Not that an MIP fee is insurmountable, but it pays to be conservative in your own valuation in case of nasty shocks!

The valuer will also recommend a figure to the lender for the cost of rebuilding your property. The lender will insist that your buildings insurance covers at least this amount and will want to see confirmation that this is in place.

Valuation fees are normally tiered; the more your home is worth, the more you'll pay.

Security

If you propose to repay the mortgage loan as part repayment, part interest-only, the lender will want to see evidence of your investment plan or life assurance policy you're using to cover the interest-only portion.

The lender may also want the policy assigned to it, although this is not as common as it once was. Assigning the rights to the lender ensures that if you try to cancel or surrender the policy, the assurance company will notify the lender. Or if you default on your mortgage payments, the lender can surrender the policy on your behalf.

Alternatively, the lender may ask you to deposit the policy with it for safekeeping. Although this doesn't transfer legal rights, it does give the lender *equal* rights to the policy – and possession is nine-tenths of the law, after all!

How good is your credit?

If you have incurred mortgage arrears, had a county court judgement (CCJ) against you, are a discharged bankrupt, or have had past credit debt, any potential lender will inevitably find out. Not that this will prevent you getting a mortgage loan. It just means your options are somewhat limited.

If you have had debt problems in the past, however minor, it is essential that you contact the credit reference agencies (see Equifax and Experian in Appendix C) for a copy of your file. All debts stay on your file for six years and you must make sure your file is correct with all cleared debts recorded. Clearing your debt will prove to the new lender that you have made the effort to fulfil your borrowing obligations.

Credit reference agencies don't actually blacklist you; they merely store information that's passed on to them from lenders and credit companies. New lenders can then access this information, and with the benefit of hindsight, decide whether to approve your application. Your file will include your listing on the electoral roll, any CCJs against you, and details of repossessions and previous loans. It will also state whether you're up to date with current loans.

Of course, any blemish means you'll be considered high-risk by the lender. If you've built up a good repayment history since the debt, it's likely that you may be able to remortgage with some of the main lenders at High Street interest rates. If you haven't, or are still in the process of clearing your debt, there are a number of specialist lenders (called 'sub-prime' lenders) who will consider you. But there's a price. Their interest rates are typically 3 per cent above the mainstream lenders' rates. And they're only likely to lend 80 per cent of your property value.

If debts haven't been cleared, your first call must be to your existing lender. You may not be offered the best rates, but even 0.5 per cent below SVR is better than the alternative.

If your existing lender is not amenable, you'll have to contact a mortgage broker. Sub-prime lenders usually only deal with customers referred to them through intermediaries. The mortgage broker may also be able to negotiate a reasonable deal for you, but take care. When you have cleared your debts and your credit rating is healthy again, you can return to normal High Street rates once more. So don't tie yourself into long preferential deals that could force you into a higher-than-normal rate after the deal ends.

Moving and borrowing more

Portability is an essential feature when you remortgage for a new loan. This is a provision in a mortgage agreement that allows you to take your mortgage with you should you move home. Otherwise, you'll be saddled with a redemption penalty.

Most lenders offer this condition as part of the mortgage package, but it's always wise to have this written into any mortgage offer.

If the lender turns you down

The lender can turn down your application for any number of reasons, and the first thing to do is discover why. The main reasons are adverse credit and current credit commitments. There's little you can do about this except apply to another lender, particularly if you're a borderline case. They all operate different credit scoring schemes, and some lenders don't have them.

Most lenders usually accept minor CCJs of between £250 and £500 provided the judgement against you has been cleared. Others accept up to £10,000. Lenders will also accept you if you have credit arrears, usually up to a limit of six months, or if you've been made bankrupt and have been discharged for more than a year.

If you are turned down through adverse credit and you're not aware of having bad debt, you'll have to check with the credit reference agencies in case you're on their file. Mistakes aren't unknown.

If you can't remortgage with a new lender, go back to your current lender and try to renegotiate better terms. Even if the deal is little better than SVR, your lender will let you switch to part repayment, part interest-only or full repayment. This may incur a small charge of around £50, but the savings you'll make alone means it's money worth spent.

Self-employed or on fixed contracts?

As more and more lenders address the changing nature of employment, they're becoming more flexible. This is good news if you're self-employed or work on fixed-term contracts.

Nevertheless, if your income tends to be irregular, remortgaging with a traditional lender could get you into financial difficulty. Fortunately, there's a solution: flexible mortgages. Although there are flaws (see Mortgages with pitfalls on page 54), this type of facility is ideal when your ability to repay your mortgage loan varies month to month.

The main point here is that you still use either the repayment method or interest-only method to repay the mortgage loan. Which means you can still make big savings by converting to full repayment or part repayment, part interest-only. The penalty is simply that you're tied to a higher interest rate than the better deals offered on the High Street.

Even so, provided you make overpayments, you can also make underpayments when your income is reduced. Better still, the mortgage providers calculate interest daily so any overpayment makes an immediate impact on the interest charged to your account. You'll need to check what the minimum overpayment is, however, as some are around £500.

Consistent overpayments, of course, will make huge savings on interest. And if you convert to full repayment, it'll knock years off your mortgage term too.

Lenders specializing in this facility are listed in Appendix A.

Lending criteria for the self-employed

If you can produce audited accounts for the past three years and provide an accountant's reference, most High Street lenders will accept your mortgage application. If you can't, there are a number of specialized lenders who only require an accountant's letter stating your taxable income. These are self-certification mortgages, whereby you provide details of your income, but you don't have to supply actual evidence such as pay slips.

First-time buyer?

As a first-time homebuyer you have most to gain from this book since most homebuyers will have already paid more for their home than was necessary. All the same, you'll need to be equally careful when selecting the right product for you. Simply put, if you have savings, you'll have the same choices as every other homebuyer. If not, you're looking at a 100 per cent or 125 per cent mortgage loan, or a cash-back deal.

Cash-back deals with a large cash component are preferable since you won't be locked into a higher interest rate than SVR. In addition, you can use the cash-back to finance all the fees you're likely to incur. Just remember that the cash-back deal is merely to get you into the housing market. There are high redemption penalties, so don't go beyond a five-year tie-in period with the lender.

Buy-to-let mortgages

Also known as let-to-buy, this type of mortgage allows you to buy another property for investment (letting) purposes. Or, if you want to move and are unable to sell your existing property or have negative equity, this facility also enables you to buy a new property using your existing property for renting out.

The least expensive way to purchase a second property is to buy it by releasing the equity (if you have plenty) in your own home. If the second property is to be used exclusively for letting, however, you'll need a buy-to-let mortgage. And the interest rates are generally higher than those on the High Street. On the other hand, unlike a normal mortgage where the maximum loan is a multiple of your gross income, buy-to-let mortgages are based on how much rent you expect the property to generate. For example, the rent might have to be 125 per cent of the monthly mortgage payment.

Alluring though purchasing and letting a second property may seem, there are a few drawbacks. Apart from higher interest rates, you'll have maintenance costs, management expenses, buildings and contents insurance, and when the property is empty, no monthly rental coming in. Rents can go up or down, and if you ever want to sell in a hurry, will you be able to? Of course, depending on location, letting could be quite a profitable investment when property is rising. And there are tax benefits too. Again, it's a question of doing the arithmetic.

STEP 4

The painless path to prosperity

How to manage your mortgage and what to do if you can't keep up repayments

Lenders come in all shapes and sizes, from those with branches in every High Street in every town in the country, to those who operate from just one central location. They all have their merits, they all offer different packages, and they all want your business. That puts you in the driving seat.

Plumping for the lender down the road may suit you if convenience is important. Equally, getting the most advantageous deal may be important even if it means setting up the mortgage through a mortgage intermediary. Whatever way you choose, make sure the deal is tailored to suit you, not the lender.

This chapter looks at how you might achieve this, and explains why building in mortgage protection could save you from losing your home through, for instance, involuntary redundancy. It also explains the steps you can take if you're struggling to meet your monthly payments. And, all about the Mortgage Code, which is sponsored by the Council of Mortgage Lenders who account for 98 per cent of residential mortgage lending in the UK.

Where to find the latest mortgage information

Although IFAs and mortgage advisers have been somewhat maligned in Step 3, they do offer some useful services. Firstly, they have access to a wide range of lenders' products and they can shop around for the most appropriate deal on your behalf.

Some of the best products are only available through intermediaries, but take care to avoid upfront fees. Most reputable intermediaries receive their commissions from the lenders, not you. Secondly, they'll do all the paperwork. And thirdly, if there are problems, they'll be able to negotiate on your behalf. You'll find their services listed in the *Yellow Pages*, and those that subscribe to the Mortgage Code can be found on a register – see Appendix C for details.

There are a number of specialist mortgage magazines available at newsagents and bookshops. These won't give you every product in the market, and can sometimes be out of date, but they usually provide best-buy tables and details of incentives and redemption periods – see Appendix D for more information. Also, check out the national press, notably Saturday's edition of the *Financial Times,* for best-buy tables.

If you have access to the Internet, the 'Slash Your Mortgage' Web site will save you a lot of time and effort. Not only is there an easy-to-use mortgage calculator to compare various mortgage types and rates, you'll also find an extensive range of mortgage products currently available from a variety of lenders. The Web site is at www.slash-mortgage.com. See Appendix D for other sites worth visiting.

Apart from that, it's a matter of contacting the lenders yourself. Appendix A lists the vast majority of lenders in the marketplace and their telephone numbers. What's more, they're listed according to the way they calculate interest, so you'll know which lenders to avoid!

Direct mortgages

Conveniently, some lenders, including many of the High Street lenders, offer to set up your mortgage over the telephone. Known as 'direct mortgages', they're usually available through mortgage providers operating from a single location. This means that their overheads tend to be lower and they can consequently offer slightly lower interest rates. Product ranges tend to be limited, however, with straightforward variable rate deals the most common. But, if you know exactly what deal you want you can shorten the application process via the telephone.

You won't be subjected to a hard sell either, and your application will be dealt with by a qualified mortgage adviser. Plus, telephone lenders are open for business until around 8 pm during the week and most are open on Saturday mornings.

You'll need a few details to hand when you call so that the lender can give you an agreement in principle. Details include an accurate valuation of your property, your earnings, National Insurance number, employer's address, bank account details, monthly personal loan and credit/charge card payments, and your current lender's details. You'll also need to know how much you want to borrow. On top of your current mortgage loan remember to add redemption penalties (if any), valuation and solicitor's fees, and if you have the equity, any additional capital you require or debts you want to consolidate.

Provided your credit assessment is satisfactory, you'll have an agreement in principle verbally followed by an offer in principle in writing. Once the forms – along with a property valuation and any other relevant documents – are returned and verified, a formal offer is issued.

'Dialling-a-mortgage' is a reasonably painless experience, and it's fast and convenient. As long as you work out beforehand precisely what you can afford to borrow (including charges and fees), arranging your mortgage over the telephone couldn't be easier. Appendix A has a list of lenders offering this service and their contact numbers.

How to avoid trouble

'In this world nothing can be said to be certain, except death and taxes', wrote Benjamin Franklin. To that, you can also add rising interest rates! It's not inconceivable that interest rates will go up sometime in the future. Neither is it inconceivable that your circumstances could change. You could be made redundant or have to stop working through illness or because of an accident. And if you're unable to make your mortgage payments to your lender, you risk losing your home. This is the last thing you want after working so hard to buy it.

When interest rates rise, most homebuyers on SVR absorb the increase in their monthly mortgage payments one way or another. Indeed, high interest rates are not the main cause of repossessions in this country. Redundancy is.

In the past, the welfare state was at hand to help you with mortgage payments. However, recent changes in state benefits have meant that financial help has all but disappeared. And you're now expected to fend for yourself.

When remortgaging, you're effectively establishing a new mortgage loan. Under new government legislation, this means you won't be eligible for certain benefits to which you might otherwise have been entitled. For instance, if your original mortgage was taken out before 2 October 1995 and you're made redundant, there's no state help for the first eight weeks. Only half your mortgage interest payments are paid for the next 18 weeks. Only after that does the state pay the full amount of mortgage interest. When you switch your mortgage loan, post-2 October 1995 rules are applied and you won't get any assistance from the state for the first 39 weeks of the claim.

The state benefit is also means tested, so you may not even qualify. If you have savings over £8,000 or your spouse or live-in partner works 24 hours or more a week, you don't qualify. If this isn't the case, the state will only meet interest payments on loans up to £100,000. And remember, there's no help with the capital portion of the loan, or any investment plan that's being used to repay the loan at the end of the term.

Mortgage insurance

Another insurance policy? Considering that you take out insurance on yourself, your family, your car and your possessions, why not mortgage payment protection? Given the choice, would you stop paying your car insurance? Probably not! Your home is the biggest asset you have, so why not protect it too?

As painful as it may seem, mortgage payment insurance is vital for protection against mortgage arrears. It's your safety net should you lose your job involuntarily or if you're unable to work through illness or disability.

It needn't be expensive, and you can cover your mortgage payments against unemployment, illness and accidents, or any combination. For the little extra every month, you'll have both security and peace of mind.

Not surprisingly, mortgage payment protection insurance could become law in the near future. For two reasons: the government wants to cut the number of people claiming benefits through redundancy; and the financial services industry – by lobbying the government for compulsory insurance – stands to gain a considerable amount from insurance policies. The government will obviously back the insurers since it complements their cost-cutting strategy of reducing income support payments.

There's the usual debate about whether mortgage insurance is a worthwhile expense. It all depends on the cost, the number of mortgage payments the policy pays out, and what exclusions are applied. Typical cost to insure against unemployment is around £4 for every £100 of monthly cover required. Protection against redundancy, accident and sickness costs around £6 for every £100 of monthly cover required.

The big danger is inappropriate insurance being sold by slick salespeople who earn lucrative commissions on the policies. For instance, if you're self-employed, permanent health insurance (PHI) is a better choice than mortgage protection insurance. It's more expensive and doesn't cover unemployment, but it insures your full income for as long as it takes you to recover. Mortgage protection insurance only lasts a year or two at most.

If you have sufficient savings, obviously mortgage insurance won't be a high priority. But if you don't, there's no doubt that mortgage insurance can prove invaluable for protecting your mortgage commitment.

If things do go wrong

Although this aspect of home buying is beyond the scope of this book, you can do a few things to help yourself if you're having difficulties making your mortgage payments.

If you are in this situation, however, priority number one is to talk to your lender. This is vitally important. Under the Mortgage Code (see below), lenders are obliged to help you resolve the problem by rearranging your payments temporarily, or permanently, to bring your mortgage account to order.

If your lender contacts *you* first, there's a good chance your credit rating will be affected. This is because lenders update the credit reference agencies every month with details of your account. Although they don't pass any opinion about your credit worthiness, the information may be used by other lenders to assess your financial history.

Of course, if you fail to make your monthly payments, the lender can exercise its right to evict you from your home through a court order. It can then sell your home to repay your mortgage debt. If you can't afford to make the full mortgage payment do not, under any circumstances, stop paying. And never simply hand back the keys. Pay what you reasonably can. That way, your lender would find it impossible to repossess your home.

Second, seek expert advice from either a specialist housing aid centre or an independent advice service such as the Citizens Advice Bureau or Shelter (see Appendix C for contact numbers). Housing aid centres are usually part of the local authority's housing department, but can be based in the consumer protection department or the welfare rights service. They will be able to advise you on whether you can apply for state benefits, and help you come to some financial arrangement with your lender.

Clearing mortgage arrears

The next step is to clear your mortgage arrears. Remember that interest will be added to the debt every month and will have to be repaid some time in the future. It's therefore advisable to enter negotiations with your lender as soon as possible and agree on a method of reducing your payments and to clear your arrears.

There are a few options available to you to clear your arrears. You can either pay a lump sum or pay off a little extra every month over an agreed period. This may sound like a tall order given that you wouldn't be in this position if your financial commitments weren't already strained!

Nevertheless, if you've remortgaged to the repayment method, either partial or full, you can extend the term of your mortgage to reduce your monthly payment. You can also pay back the arrears by asking your lender to add it onto the capital you still owe to create a new mortgage.

Alternatively, if you've switched from an interest-only mortgage and your investment plan is still running, consider selling or surrendering it to raise the capital you need to repay the arrears, and if possible, reduce your mortgage balance. If your mortgage is part repayment, part interest-only you'll have to switch to full repayment. You'll have to ask your lender to agree to this as, in the case of endowments, the policy may be assigned to the lender.

The Mortgage Code

The Mortgage Code is a voluntary code of practice with which members of the Council of Mortgage Lenders (CML) comply. It provides protection for you as a borrower and sets out the minimum standards that both lenders and mortgage intermediaries have to meet. If a member fails to meet the standards of the code, and you suffer as a result, you have the right to compensation under a compulsory independent complaints scheme.

Briefly, the code sets out:

- ☐ how your mortgage should be arranged;
- ☐ what information you should receive before you commit yourself; and
- ☐ how your mortgage should be dealt with once it is in place.

What this means is that the lender or intermediary must tell you a whole raft of details (most of which are covered in Appendix A – Checklist) about the mortgage you're considering.

If you're using a mortgage intermediary, the intermediary must also tell you how much he or she is receiving from the lender for arranging your mortgage. The intermediary must also tell you whether he or she uses a panel of selected lenders, or reviews the market as a whole.

If you want more details on the code, you'll find the address and telephone number of the CML in Appendix C, and its Web site address in Appendix D.

Appendix A – The inquisition

A comprehensive list of lenders in the marketplace, their contact numbers, and how they calculate the interest on your mortgage. Plus there's a checklist to use when interviewing them so you know precisely what the deals offer

All the lenders listed in the following pages (with a few exceptions) belong to the Council of Mortgage Lenders (CML). This means they all subscribe to the Code of Mortgage Lending Practice. Although it's a voluntary code, an independent review body monitors the business practice of the members to ensure compliance with the code.

In addition, lenders must also be a member of one of the recognized complaints schemes (see Appendix C for more information). This offers a fair degree of protection should you have a complaint against the lender. And if you suffer as a result of the member failing to keep to the code, compensation of up to £100,000 can be awarded.

There are many more lenders and intermediaries in the marketplace providing dependable and responsible services and who offer ethical advice. If you decide to use them rather than an organization with the CML, at least you do so knowingly – forewarned is forearmed as they say!

Accounting methods used by the lenders

This may come as a surprise to you, but lenders calculate the interest owed on repayment mortgages in different ways. And it can result in large differences in the overall cost of the mortgage over the term. What shouldn't surprise you, however, is that the most common method works in the lender's favour, not the borrower's. Indeed, it's estimated that lenders will receive more than £70 billion extra in interest over the next 25 years using one particular scheme.

For interest-only mortgages, since there's no capital being paid over the term, it doesn't matter what scheme the lender adopts. It only matters if you intend making a capital payment.

The three most common accounting schemes adopted by the lenders are 'annual rest', 'monthly rest' and 'daily rest'.

Annual rest

The vast majority of lenders use this method. Interest is debited to your account at the start of the lender's accounting year and your mortgage payments are set against it.

Each monthly mortgage payment you make has no impact on the amount of interest you are charged during that year. It's only at the end of the lender's accounting year (and it's not necessarily 31 December) that your 12 monthly payments, less interest charged, are used to reduce the interest for the following year. Using this method, the lender effectively receives a 12-month interest-free loan from you.

If you make an additional capital payment in advance of the lender's accounting year, the amount of interest chargeable in the following year is reduced. This also applies to interest-only mortgages. The lender, though, must be notified that the additional payment is to be applied to the capital, otherwise it is treated as an interest overpayment and will not be used to reduce your capital balance.

Monthly rest

This scheme can make a surprising difference to how much you'll pay back over the term compared to the annual rest scheme. In essence, each time you make a payment, your capital balance is adjusted and interest is debited to your account every month. Since your payment counts toward reducing the interest owed each month, the faster your mortgage is repaid.

Lenders adopting this method factor this in when they calculate your monthly mortgage payment, so while your 25-year term remains the same, you simply pay less per month compared to a mortgage under the annual rest scheme.

Daily rest

This scheme operates in a similar way to monthly rest (and credit cards), but interest is debited to your account every day rather than every month.

You may think that this scheme will make even more savings over and above those made using the monthly rest scheme. Actually, it doesn't. The reason is that if you pay your mortgage monthly, that is, one payment per calendar month, you can't take advantage of the daily interest adjustment. Used in this way, it's the equivalent of the monthly rest scheme.

The only way to benefit from this scheme is to make your mortgage payments weekly or fortnightly. Even then, savings will be minimal (relative to monthly rest) since each payment is only a fraction of the normal monthly payment.

How much can you save?

Here are some examples of how much you can save under monthly and daily rest schemes *relative to* the annual rest scheme.

Let's assume a £50,000 repayment mortgage over 25 years, at an average interest rate over this term of 7 per cent. The cost per month is £358 under the annual rest scheme.

Keeping the same monthly payments, under the monthly rest scheme you would save £3,370 in interest and you'd repay the loan nine months earlier.

Now, keeping the same monthly payments, but paying half at the beginning of the month and half in the middle of the month, using the daily rest scheme would save you £3,510 in interest and you'd repay the loan 10 months earlier.

If the interest rate averaged 10 per cent over the 25-year term, the savings are more significant. In this case, under monthly rest, you would save £6,220 in interest and you'd repay the loan 13 months earlier. Under daily rest, you would save £6,490 in interest and you'd repay the loan 13½ months earlier.

The figures above are merely an illustration of what the savings would be when mortgage payments are the same but interest is calculated using the various schemes. In reality, if you remortgage with a lender operating either the monthly or daily rest schemes, your actual monthly payment is less than that of a lender offering the equivalent interest rate but using the annual rest scheme. The actual figures that are used are given in Appendix B.

For example, let's assume a £50,000 repayment mortgage over 25 years, at an average interest rate over this term of 7 per cent. The cost per month is £358 per month under the annual rest scheme, and £354 under the monthly or daily rest scheme. This results in a saving of £1,260 using the monthly or daily rest scheme.

You may be wondering why the savings aren't the same as those in the first example above. The reason is you're paying *less* every month (that is, not the same amount), therefore, less is being applied to the capital to reduce the mortgage balance over the term. Indeed, the first example just goes to show the power of what paying £4 extra a month does to your mortgage balance! If those lenders who provide flexible mortgages ever offer similar low-interest deals as the mainstream lenders, this would be the type of mortgage to go for!

Lenders using the annual rest scheme

The names of the lenders listed below are not necessarily the full legal title of each organization. (*Denotes the lender is not a member of the CML at time of writing.)

Abbey National plc – (0171) 612 4000
Alliance and Leicester – (0171) 629 6661
Barclays Bank plc – (0113) 296 5600
Barnsley Building Society – (01226) 733 999
Bath Investment and Building Society – (01225) 423 271
Beverly Building Society – (01482) 881 510
Bradford and Bingley Building Society – (01274) 555 555
Bristol and West plc – (0117) 979 2222
Britannia Building Society – (01538) 399 399
Buckinghamshire Building Society – (01494) 873 064
Cambridge Building Society – (01223) 727 727
Catholic Building Society – (0171) 222 6736
Cheltenham and Gloucester plc – (01452) 372 372
Cheshire Building Society – (01625) 613 612
Clay Cross Building Society – (01246) 862 120
Coventry Building Society – (01203) 555 255
Cumberland Building Society – (01228) 541 341
Darlington Building Society – (01325) 366 366
Derbyshire Building Society – (01332) 841 000
Dudley Building Society – (01384) 231 414
Dunfermline Building Society – (01383) 627 727
Earl Shilton Building Society – (01455) 844 422
Ecology Building Society, The – (01535) 635 933
Gainsborough Building Society – (01427) 611 011
Halifax plc – (01422) 333 333
Hanley Economic Building Society – (01782) 255 000
Harpenden Building Society – (01582) 765 411
Holmesdale Building Society – (01737) 245 716

Ipswich Building Society – (01473) 211 021
Lambeth Building Society – (0171) 928 1331
Leeds and Holbeck Building Society – (0113) 225 2000
Leek United Building Society – (01538) 384 151
Loughborough Building Society – (01509) 610 707
Manchester Building Society – (0161) 833 8888
Mansfield Building Society, The – (01623) 649 921
Market Harborough Building Society – (01858) 463 244
Marsden Building Society – (01282) 440 500
Melton Mowbray Building Society – (01664) 563 937
Money Store, The – (0171) 512 4006
Monmouthshire Building Society – (01633) 840 454
National Counties Building Society – (01372) 742 211
Nationwide Building Society – (01793) 513 513
NatWest Mortgage Services – (0121) 234 3000
Newbury Building Society – (01635) 43676
Newcastle Building Society – (0191) 244 2000
Northern Rock plc – (0191) 285 7191
Norwich and Peterborough Building Society – (01733) 372 372
Nottingham Building Society – (0115) 948 1444
Nottingham Imperial Building Society – (0115) 981 7220
Portman Building Society – (01202) 292 444
Principality Building Society – (01222) 344 188
Progressive Building Society (N. Ireland) – (01232) 244 926
Saffron Walden Herts and Essex Building Society – (01799) 522 211
Scarborough Building Society – (01723) 368 155
Scottish Building Society – (0131) 220 1111
Shipshed Building Society – (01509) 503 302
Skipton Building Society – (01756) 700 500
Stafford Railway Building Society, The – (01785) 223 212
Staffordshire Building Society – (01902) 317 317
Standard Building Society, The – (0191) 257 4123
Stroud and Swindon Building Society – (01453) 757 011
Swansea Building Society – (01792) 641 155
Teachers' Building Society – (01202) 887 171
Tipton and Coseley Building Society – (0121) 557 2551
United Bank of Kuwait plc, The – (0171) 487 6500

Universal Building Society – (0191) 232 0973
West Bromwich Building Society – (0121) 525 7070
Woolwich plc – (0181) 298 5000
Yorkshire Building Society – (01274) 740 740

Lenders using the quarterly rest scheme

Bank of Cyprus (London) Ltd – (0171) 304 5800
Paragon Group of Companies plc – (0121) 712 2323

Lenders using the monthly or daily rest scheme

Allchurches Mortgage Company Ltd – (01452) 526 265
Allied Irish Bank (GB) – (01895) 272 222
Bank of Ireland Home Mortgages Ltd – (0881) 939 3393
Bank of Scotland – (0131) 317 6601
Birmingham Midshires Building Society – (01902) 302 000
Capital Homes Loans Ltd – (01252) 365 800
Chelsea Building Society – (01242) 271 271
Chesham Building Society – (01494) 782 575
Chorley and District Building Society, The – (01257) 279 373
Clydesdale Bank – (0141) 248 7070
First Active Financial plc – (0800) 550 551
Furness Building Society – (01229) 824 560
Hinckley and Rugby Building Society – (01455) 251 234
Household Mortgage Corporation Ltd – (01494) 459 100
Irish Permanent plc (N. Ireland) – (03531) 661 5577
Kensington Mortgage Company – (0990) 561 020

Kent Reliance Building Society – (01634) 848 944
Legal and General Bank Ltd – (0870) 010 0338
Lloyds TSB – (0131) 225 4555
Mercantile Building Society – (0191) 295 9500
Midland Bank plc – (0171) 260 7847
Mortgage Business plc, The – (01244) 694 823
Mortgage Express Ltd – (0181) 449 8888
*Mortgage Trust – (0800) 550 551
Northern Bank Ltd (N. Ireland) – (01232) 245 277
Penrith Building Society – (01768) 863 675
Royal Bank of Scotland plc, The – (01475) 551 036
Sainsbury's Bank plc – (0131) 442 5022
Scottish Widows Bank plc – (0845) 845 0829
Southern Pacific Mortgages Ltd – (0171) 590 1500
Standard Life Bank – (0845) 845 8450
Sun Bank plc – (01438) 744 500
*UCB Home Loans – (0645) 401 400
Vernon Building Society – (0161) 429 6262
Wesleyan Home Loans – (0121) 200 3003
Woolwich Direct – (0345) 454 546
Yorkshire Bank – (0113) 247 2000

Flexible mortgages

Alliance and Leicester – (0845) 303 3000
Bank of Scotland – (0131) 317 6601
Clydesdale Bank – (0800) 419 000
Coventry Building Society – (0845) 766 5522
*Direct Line – See *Yellow Pages*
*Egg – (0845) 600 0290
First Active (Eire) – (0800) 550 551
*First Direct – (0800) 24 24 24
Furness Building Society – (0800) 834 312
Household Mortgage Corporation Ltd – (01494) 459 100

Legal and General Bank Ltd – (0870) 010 0338
Manchester Building Society – (0161) 833 8888
Market Harborough Building Society – (01858) 463 244
Mortgage Business plc, The – (0345) 253 253
Mortgage Express Ltd – (0500) 050 020
Royal Bank of Scotland plc, The – (0800) 121 21
Sainsbury's Bank plc – (0500) 700 600
Scottish Widows Bank plc – (0845) 829 829
Standard Life Bank – (0845) 845 8450
Stroud and Swindon Building Society – (0800) 616 112
Sun Bank plc – (01438) 744 505
Swansea Building Society – (01792) 641 155
Tipton and Coseley Building Society – (0800) 833 853
*UCB Home Loans – (0645) 401 400
Vernon Building Society – (0161) 429 6262
*Virgin Direct – (08456) 000 001
Woolwich plc – (0845) 607 6666
Yorkshire Bank – (0800) 202 122

Direct mortgages

Abbey National Direct – (0800) 555 100
Alliance and Leicester – (0500) 83 83 83
Bank of Scotland Mortgages Direct – (0800) 810 810
Barclays Bank plc – (0800) 400 121
Bradford and Bingley Building Society – (0345) 852 852
Bristol and West plc – (0800) 119955
Britannia Building Society – (0800) 526 350
Chelsea Direct – (0800) 291 291
Cheltenham and Gloucester Direct – (0800) 731 8511
Derbyshire Direct – (01332) 207 666
*Direct Line – See *Yellow Pages*
*First Direct – (0345) 100 103
*First Mortgage – (0800) 080 088

Furness Building Society – (0800) 834 312
Halifax plc – (0800) 101 110
Hinckley and Rugby Building Society – (0800) 774 499
Household Mortgage Corporation Ltd – (01494) 459 100
Kensington Mortgage Company – (0800) 111 020
Lambeth Building Society – (0800) 225 221
Leeds and Holbeck Building Society – (0800) 072 5726
Legal and General Mortgages Direct – (0800) 664 444
Market Harborough Building Society – (01858) 463 244
Midland Bank plc – (0800) 881 155
Money Store, The – (0800) 783 4448
Mortgage Business plc, The – (0345) 253 253
Mortgage Express Ltd – (0500) 050 020
*Mortgage Trust – (0800) 550 551
Nationwide Direct – (0800) 302 010
NatWest Mortgage Services – (0800) 400 999
Newcastle Direct – (0191) 244 2468
Northern Rock plc – (0845) 605 0500
Paragon Group of Companies plc – (0121) 712 2323
Principality Building Society – (0800) 163 817
Sainsbury's Bank plc – (0500) 700 600
Scottish Widows Bank plc – (0845) 829 829
*UCB Direct – (0500) 401 400
*Virgin Direct – (08456) 000 001
Woolwich Direct – (0345) 454 546

Checklist

Listed below are some of the most important questions to ask potential lenders when remortgaging. You can of course ask the same questions of your own lender if you are considering remortgaging with it.

The quickest way to find out which deals are available to you is to telephone the lenders first. Even if the headline products are not available, there are usually plenty of others in their portfolio. If you can't make up your mind or don't know what deal to choose, contact some mortgage intermediaries for advice. You'll get a list of intermediaries in your local *Yellow Pages*. Remember that most use a panel of lenders so just contacting one might not provide you with the best deal available.

- ☐ How is interest calculated and charged?
- ☐ What is the maximum advance to property value?
- ☐ Do you charge an MIP, and if so, what is the minimum loan-to-value ratio?
- ☐ What is the income multiplier?
- ☐ How much is the arrangement fee?
- ☐ How much are the legal fees?
- ☐ How much is the valuation fee?
- ☐ Are any of the fees refunded on completion?
- ☐ Is the mortgage portable?
- ☐ Are there any compulsory insurances?
- ☐ How long is the redemption period?
- ☐ How is the early redemption penalty calculated?
- ☐ Is early redemption charged at the prevailing standard variable rate?
- ☐ Are additional payments allowed during the lock-in period?
- ☐ Are there charges for part redemption?
- ☐ How much will it cost to fully repay the mortgage loan?

Appendix B – Be calculating and save

Tables to help you work out how much you'll pay per month on both repayment (including annual and monthly/daily rest) and interest-only mortgages for interest rates between 15 per cent and 1 per cent

The following tables will enable you to calculate your monthly mortgage payments for a whole range of scenarios. Whether you want to split your mortgage as part repayment, part interest-only or switch to full repayment and reduce your mortgage term, you'll get an accurate indication of just how much it will cost. And you'll be able to work out how much you'll save a month if you decide to go for a discount, fixed or capped product.

The calculations are easy but you will need a calculator!

How to calculate your monthly payment

Part repayment, part interest-only

To find out how much you'll pay per month, first go to the page that has the same term remaining as your investment plan. For example, if your plan matures in 2020, go to *Term remaining: 21 years*. Then:

1. Locate the interest rate closest to the rate you're on now.
2. Depending on how the lender calculates interest, match the interest rate in step 1 to the cost-per-£1,000 rate for the repayment portion of your mortgage. For example, if your current interest rate is 7.25 per cent with 21 years to term and the lender calculates interest using the monthly rest or daily rest method, the cost per £1,000 is £7.7358.
3. Multiply this figure by the number of £1,000s you want on repayment. For example, if you want to keep £30,000 from your investment plan, multiply the cost per £1,000 by 30. Using the cost-per-£1,000 rate in step 2, this works out as £232.07 per month.
4. For the same rate of interest, now calculate the cost per month for the interest-only portion of the mortgage. At 7.25 per cent, the cost per £1,000 is £6.0417. Multiply this figure by the number of thousands that are to remain as interest-only. If you intend keeping say £20,000 as interest-only, multiply £6.0417 by 20. This gives you a monthly cost of £120.83.
5. Add the repayment cost to the interest-only cost to reveal your new monthly payment. In this example, it's £352.90.

Full repayment

To find out how much you'll pay per month by switching to full repayment, first go to the page that has the same term remaining as your current mortgage. Alternatively, if your intention is to reduce the number of years of your mortgage term, go to the page with that term. For example, if your mortgage finishes in 2020, go to *Term remaining: 21 years*. If you want to reduce your term by five years, go to *Term remaining: 16 years*. Then follow steps 1, 2 and 3 above.

For example, say the interest rate is 7.25 per cent and you have £49,500 on repayment. If you want to reduce the mortgage term from 21 years to 16 years using a lender operating the monthly or daily rest scheme, simply multiply the cost-per-£1,000 rate of £8.8118 (16 years) by 49.5 to get your new monthly payment of £436.18.

Term remaining: 5 years

Interest Rate	Repayment Mortgage Cost-per-£1,000		Interest-only Mortgage
	Annual Rest	Monthly/Daily Rest	Cost-per-£1,000
15.00%	24.8596	23.7786	12.5000
14.75%	24.7126	23.6475	12.2917
14.50%	24.5660	23.5168	12.0833
14.25%	24.4196	23.3865	11.8750
14.00%	24.2736	23.2566	11.6667
13.75%	24.1279	23.1272	11.4583
13.50%	23.9826	22.9981	11.2500
13.25%	23.8376	22.8694	11.0417
13.00%	23.6929	22.7412	10.8333
12.75%	23.5485	22.6133	10.6250
12.50%	23.4045	22.4859	10.4167
12.25%	23.2608	22.3588	10.2083
12.00%	23.1175	22.2322	10.0000
11.75%	22.9745	22.1060	9.7917
11.50%	22.8318	21.9802	9.5833
11.25%	22.6895	21.8548	9.3750
11.00%	22.5475	21.7298	9.1667
10.75%	22.4059	21.6053	8.9583
10.50%	22.2646	21.4812	8.7500
10.25%	22.1237	21.3574	8.5417
10.00%	21.9831	21.2341	8.3333
9.75%	21.8429	21.1112	8.1250
9.50%	21.7030	20.9888	7.9167
9.25%	21.5635	20.8667	7.7083
9.00%	21.4244	20.7451	7.5000
8.75%	21.2856	20.6239	7.2917
8.50%	21.1471	20.5031	7.0833
8.25%	21.0091	20.3827	6.8750
8.00%	20.8714	20.2628	6.6667
7.75%	20.7340	20.1433	6.4583
7.50%	20.5971	20.0242	6.2500
7.25%	20.4605	19.9055	6.0417
7.00%	20.3242	19.7872	5.8333

Term remaining: 5 years continued

Interest Rate	Repayment Mortgage Cost-per-£1,000		Interest-only Mortgage
	Annual Rest	Monthly/Daily Rest	Cost-per-£1,000
6.75%	20.1884	19.6694	5.6250
6.50%	20.0529	19.5520	5.4167
6.25%	19.9178	19.4350	5.2083
6.00%	19.7830	19.3185	5.0000
5.75%	19.6487	19.2023	4.7917
5.50%	19.5147	19.0866	4.5833
5.25%	19.3811	18.9714	4.3750
5.00%	19.2479	18.8565	4.1667
4.75%	19.1151	18.7421	3.9583
4.50%	18.9826	18.6281	3.7500
4.25%	18.8506	18.5146	3.5417
4.00%	18.7189	18.4014	3.3333
3.75%	18.5877	18.2887	3.1250
3.50%	18.4568	18.1765	2.9167
3.25%	18.3263	18.0646	2.7083
3.00%	18.1962	17.9532	2.5000
2.75%	18.0665	17.8422	2.2917
2.50%	17.9372	17.7317	2.0833
2.25%	17.8084	17.6216	1.8750
2.00%	17.6799	17.5119	1.6667
1.00%	17.1700	17.0775	0.8333

Term remaining: 6 years

Interest Rate	Repayment Mortgage Cost-per-£1,000		Interest-only Mortgage Cost-per-£1,000
	Annual Rest	Monthly/Daily Rest	
15.00%	22.0197	21.1364	12.5000
14.75%	21.8717	21.0008	12.2917
14.50%	21.7240	20.8656	12.0833
14.25%	21.5767	20.7310	11.8750
14.00%	21.4298	20.5968	11.6667
13.75%	21.2833	20.4631	11.4583
13.50%	21.1372	20.3299	11.2500
13.25%	20.9914	20.1971	11.0417
13.00%	20.8461	20.0649	10.8333
12.75%	20.7012	19.9331	10.6250
12.50%	20.5566	19.8018	10.4167
12.25%	20.4125	19.6710	10.2083
12.00%	20.2688	19.5406	10.0000
11.75%	20.1255	19.4108	9.7917
11.50%	19.9826	19.2814	9.5833
11.25%	19.8401	19.1526	9.3750
11.00%	19.6980	19.0242	9.1667
10.75%	19.5564	18.8963	8.9583
10.50%	19.4152	18.7689	8.7500
10.25%	19.2743	18.6420	8.5417
10.00%	19.1339	18.5156	8.3333
9.75%	18.9940	18.3897	8.1250
9.50%	18.8544	18.2643	7.9167
9.25%	18.7153	18.1394	7.7083
9.00%	18.5766	18.0150	7.5000
8.75%	18.4384	17.8911	7.2917
8.50%	18.3006	17.7677	7.0833
8.25%	18.1632	17.6448	6.8750
8.00%	18.0263	17.5224	6.6667
7.75%	17.8898	17.4005	6.4583
7.50%	17.7537	17.2791	6.2500
7.25%	17.6181	17.1582	6.0417
7.00%	17.4830	17.0378	5.8333

Term remaining: 6 years continued

Interest Rate	Repayment Mortgage Cost-per-£1,000		Interest-only Mortgage
	Annual Rest	Monthly/Daily Rest	Cost-per-£1,000
6.75%	17.3483	16.9179	5.6250
6.50%	17.2140	16.7985	5.4167
6.25%	17.0802	16.6797	5.2083
6.00%	16.9469	16.5613	5.0000
5.75%	16.8140	16.4435	4.7917
5.50%	16.6816	16.3261	4.5833
5.25%	16.5496	16.2093	4.3750
5.00%	16.4181	16.0930	4.1667
4.75%	16.2871	15.9772	3.9583
4.50%	16.1565	15.8619	3.7500
4.25%	16.0264	15.7471	3.5417
4.00%	15.8968	15.6329	3.3333
3.75%	15.7677	15.5191	3.1250
3.50%	15.6390	15.4059	2.9167
3.25%	15.5108	15.2932	2.7083
3.00%	15.3831	15.1810	2.5000
2.75%	15.2559	15.0693	2.2917
2.50%	15.1292	14.9581	2.0833
2.25%	15.0029	14.8475	1.8750
2.00%	14.8772	14.7374	1.6667
1.00%	14.3790	14.3020	0.8333

Term remaining: 7 years

Interest Rate	Repayment Mortgage Cost-per-£1,000		Interest-only Mortgage
	Annual Rest	Monthly/Daily Rest	Cost-per-£1,000
15.00%	20.0300	19.2900	12.5000
14.75%	19.8800	19.1499	12.2917
14.50%	19.7305	19.0104	12.0833
14.25%	19.5814	18.8714	11.8750
14.00%	19.4327	18.7329	11.6667
13.75%	19.2845	18.5950	11.4583
13.50%	19.1367	18.4577	11.2500
13.25%	18.9894	18.3209	11.0417
13.00%	18.8426	18.1846	10.8333
12.75%	18.6962	18.0489	10.6250
12.50%	18.5503	17.9137	10.4167
12.25%	18.4048	17.7791	10.2083
12.00%	18.2598	17.6451	10.0000
11.75%	18.1153	17.5116	9.7917
11.50%	17.9713	17.3787	9.5833
11.25%	17.8277	17.2463	9.3750
11.00%	17.6846	17.1145	9.1667
10.75%	17.5420	16.9832	8.9583
10.50%	17.3999	16.8526	8.7500
10.25%	17.2583	16.7225	8.5417
10.00%	17.1171	16.5929	8.3333
9.75%	16.9765	16.4639	8.1250
9.50%	16.8363	16.3356	7.9167
9.25%	16.6967	16.2077	7.7083
9.00%	16.5575	16.0805	7.5000
8.75%	16.4189	15.9538	7.2917
8.50%	16.2808	15.8277	7.0833
8.25%	16.1431	15.7022	6.8750
8.00%	16.0060	15.5773	6.6667
7.75%	15.8694	15.4529	6.4583
7.50%	15.7334	15.3292	6.2500
7.25%	15.5978	15.2060	6.0417
7.00%	15.4628	15.0834	5.8333

Term remaining: 7 years continued

Interest Rate	Repayment Mortgage Cost-per-£1,000 Annual Rest	Repayment Mortgage Cost-per-£1,000 Monthly/Daily Rest	Interest-only Mortgage Cost-per-£1,000
6.75%	15.3283	14.9614	5.6250
6.50%	15.1943	14.8400	5.4167
6.25%	15.0608	14.7192	5.2083
6.00%	14.9279	14.5989	5.0000
5.75%	14.7955	14.4793	4.7917
5.50%	14.6637	14.3603	4.5833
5.25%	14.5324	14.2418	4.3750
5.00%	14.4017	14.1239	4.1667
4.75%	14.2714	14.0067	3.9583
4.50%	14.1418	13.8900	3.7500
4.25%	14.0127	13.7739	3.5417
4.00%	13.8841	13.6585	3.3333
3.75%	13.7561	13.5436	3.1250
3.50%	13.6287	13.4293	2.9167
3.25%	13.5018	13.3157	2.7083
3.00%	13.3755	13.2026	2.5000
2.75%	13.2498	13.0901	2.2917
2.50%	13.1246	12.9783	2.0833
2.25%	13.0000	12.8670	1.8750
2.00%	12.8760	12.7563	1.6667
1.00%	12.3857	12.3197	0.8333

Term remaining: 8 years

Interest Rate	Repayment Mortgage Cost-per-£1,000		Interest-only Mortgage
	Annual Rest	Monthly/Daily Rest	Cost-per-£1,000
15.00%	18.5708	17.9400	12.5000
14.75%	18.4184	17.7955	12.2917
14.50%	18.2665	17.6517	12.0833
14.25%	18.1151	17.5084	11.8750
14.00%	17.9642	17.3658	11.6667
13.75%	17.8138	17.2238	11.4583
13.50%	17.6638	17.0823	11.2500
13.25%	17.5144	16.9415	11.0417
13.00%	17.3656	16.8013	10.8333
12.75%	17.2172	16.6617	10.6250
12.50%	17.0693	16.5227	10.4167
12.25%	16.9220	16.3843	10.2083
12.00%	16.7752	16.2466	10.0000
11.75%	16.6290	16.1095	9.7917
11.50%	16.4833	15.9730	9.5833
11.25%	16.3381	15.8371	9.3750
11.00%	16.1934	15.7019	9.1667
10.75%	16.0493	15.5673	8.9583
10.50%	15.9058	15.4333	8.7500
10.25%	15.7628	15.3000	8.5417
10.00%	15.6203	15.1673	8.3333
9.75%	15.4785	15.0353	8.1250
9.50%	15.3371	14.9039	7.9167
9.25%	15.1964	14.7731	7.7083
9.00%	15.0562	14.6431	7.5000
8.75%	14.9166	14.5136	7.2917
8.50%	14.7776	14.3848	7.0833
8.25%	14.6391	14.2567	6.8750
8.00%	14.5012	14.1292	6.6667
7.75%	14.3639	14.0024	6.4583
7.50%	14.2273	13.8762	6.2500
7.25%	14.0912	13.7507	6.0417
7.00%	13.9556	13.6259	5.8333

Term remaining: 8 years continued

Interest Rate	Repayment Mortgage Cost-per-£1,000		Interest-only Mortgage
	Annual Rest	Monthly/Daily Rest	Cost-per-£1,000
6.75%	13.8207	13.5018	5.6250
6.50%	13.6864	13.3783	5.4167
6.25%	13.5527	13.2554	5.2083
6.00%	13.4197	13.1333	5.0000
5.75%	13.2872	13.0118	4.7917
5.50%	13.1553	12.8910	4.5833
5.25%	13.0241	12.7709	4.3750
5.00%	12.8935	12.6514	4.1667
4.75%	12.7635	12.5327	3.9583
4.50%	12.6341	12.4146	3.7500
4.25%	12.5054	12.2971	3.5417
4.00%	12.3773	12.1804	3.3333
3.75%	12.2499	12.0644	3.1250
3.50%	12.1231	11.9490	2.9167
3.25%	11.9969	11.8343	2.7083
3.00%	11.8714	11.7203	2.5000
2.75%	11.7465	11.6070	2.2917
2.50%	11.6223	11.4944	2.0833
2.25%	11.4987	11.3825	1.8750
2.00%	11.3758	11.2713	1.6667
1.00%	10.8909	10.8332	0.8333

Term remaining: 9 years

Interest Rate	Repayment Mortgage Cost-per-£1,000		Interest-only Mortgage Cost-per-£1,000
	Annual Rest	Monthly/Daily Rest	
15.00%	17.4645	16.9199	12.5000
14.75%	17.3094	16.7712	12.2917
14.50%	17.1548	16.6232	12.0833
14.25%	17.0008	16.4758	11.8750
14.00%	16.8474	16.3290	11.6667
13.75%	16.6945	16.1829	11.4583
13.50%	16.5421	16.0375	11.2500
13.25%	16.3903	15.8928	11.0417
13.00%	16.2391	15.7487	10.8333
12.75%	16.0884	15.6052	10.6250
12.50%	15.9383	15.4625	10.4167
12.25%	15.7888	15.3204	10.2083
12.00%	15.6399	15.1790	10.0000
11.75%	15.4916	15.0383	9.7917
11.50%	15.3438	14.8983	9.5833
11.25%	15.1967	14.7590	9.3750
11.00%	15.0501	14.6204	9.1667
10.75%	14.9042	14.4825	8.9583
10.50%	14.7589	14.3453	8.7500
10.25%	14.6141	14.2087	8.5417
10.00%	14.4700	14.0729	8.3333
9.75%	14.3266	13.9378	8.1250
9.50%	14.1837	13.8035	7.9167
9.25%	14.0415	13.6698	7.7083
9.00%	13.8999	13.5369	7.5000
8.75%	13.7590	13.4046	7.2917
8.50%	13.6186	13.2732	7.0833
8.25%	13.4790	13.1424	6.8750
8.00%	13.3400	13.0124	6.6667
7.75%	13.2016	12.8831	6.4583
7.50%	13.0639	12.7545	6.2500
7.25%	12.9269	12.6267	6.0417
7.00%	12.7905	12.4996	5.8333

Term remaining: 9 years continued

Interest Rate	Repayment Mortgage Cost-per-£1,000		Interest-only Mortgage Cost-per-£1,000
	Annual Rest	Monthly/Daily Rest	
6.75%	12.6548	12.3733	5.6250
6.50%	12.5198	12.2477	5.4167
6.25%	12.3855	12.1228	5.2083
6.00%	12.2519	11.9987	5.0000
5.75%	12.1189	11.8754	4.7917
5.50%	11.9866	11.7528	4.5833
5.25%	11.8550	11.6310	4.3750
5.00%	11.7242	11.5099	4.1667
4.75%	11.5940	11.3896	3.9583
4.50%	11.4645	11.2701	3.7500
4.25%	11.3358	11.1513	3.5417
4.00%	11.2077	11.0333	3.3333
3.75%	11.0804	10.9160	3.1250
3.50%	10.9538	10.7995	2.9167
3.25%	10.8280	10.6838	2.7083
3.00%	10.7028	10.5689	2.5000
2.75%	10.5784	10.4547	2.2917
2.50%	10.4547	10.3413	2.0833
2.25%	10.3318	10.2287	1.8750
2.00%	10.2096	10.1168	1.6667
1.00%	9.7284	9.6772	0.8333

Term remaining: 10 years

Interest Rate	Repayment Mortgage Cost-per-£1,000		Interest-only Mortgage Cost-per-£1,000
	Annual Rest	Monthly/Daily Rest	
15.00%	16.6043	16.1299	12.5000
14.75%	16.4464	15.9771	12.2917
14.50%	16.2891	15.8249	12.0833
14.25%	16.1323	15.6735	11.8750
14.00%	15.9761	15.5228	11.6667
13.75%	15.8206	15.3728	11.4583
13.50%	15.6656	15.2235	11.2500
13.25%	15.5112	15.0749	11.0417
13.00%	15.3575	14.9270	10.8333
12.75%	15.2043	14.7798	10.6250
12.50%	15.0518	14.6334	10.4167
12.25%	14.8999	14.4877	10.2083
12.00%	14.7487	14.3427	10.0000
11.75%	14.5981	14.1985	9.7917
11.50%	14.4481	14.0551	9.5833
11.25%	14.2988	13.9124	9.3750
11.00%	14.1501	13.7704	9.1667
10.75%	14.0021	13.6292	8.9583
10.50%	13.8548	13.4888	8.7500
10.25%	13.7081	13.3491	8.5417
10.00%	13.5621	13.2102	8.3333
9.75%	13.4168	13.0721	8.1250
9.50%	13.2722	12.9347	7.9167
9.25%	13.1282	12.7982	7.7083
9.00%	12.9850	12.6624	7.5000
8.75%	12.8425	12.5274	7.2917
8.50%	12.7006	12.3933	7.0833
8.25%	12.5595	12.2599	6.8750
8.00%	12.4191	12.1273	6.6667
7.75%	12.2794	11.9955	6.4583
7.50%	12.1405	11.8646	6.2500
7.25%	12.0023	11.7344	6.0417
7.00%	11.8648	11.6051	5.8333

Term remaining: 10 years continued

Interest Rate	Repayment Mortgage Cost-per-£1,000		Interest-only Mortgage Cost-per-£1,000
	Annual Rest	Monthly/Daily Rest	
6.75%	11.7281	11.4766	5.6250
6.50%	11.5921	11.3489	5.4167
6.25%	11.4568	11.2220	5.2083
6.00%	11.3223	11.0959	5.0000
5.75%	11.1886	10.9707	4.7917
5.50%	11.0556	10.8464	4.5833
5.25%	10.9235	10.7228	4.3750
5.00%	10.7920	10.6001	4.1667
4.75%	10.6614	10.4782	3.9583
4.50%	10.5316	10.3572	3.7500
4.25%	10.4025	10.2371	3.5417
4.00%	10.2742	10.1177	3.3333
3.75%	10.1468	9.9992	3.1250
3.50%	10.0201	9.8816	2.9167
3.25%	9.8943	9.7648	2.7083
3.00%	9.7692	9.6489	2.5000
2.75%	9.6450	9.5339	2.2917
2.50%	9.5216	9.4196	2.0833
2.25%	9.3990	9.3063	1.8750
2.00%	9.2772	9.1938	1.6667
1.00%	8.7985	8.7525	0.8333

Term remaining: 11 years

Interest Rate	Repayment Mortgage Cost-per-£1,000		Interest-only Mortgage Cost-per-£1,000
	Annual Rest	Monthly/Daily Rest	
15.00%	15.9224	15.5061	12.5000
14.75%	15.7616	15.3494	12.2917
14.50%	15.6014	15.1933	12.0833
14.25%	15.4418	15.0380	11.8750
14.00%	15.2829	14.8834	11.6667
13.75%	15.1245	14.7296	11.4583
13.50%	14.9669	14.5765	11.2500
13.25%	14.8098	14.4242	11.0417
13.00%	14.6535	14.2727	10.8333
12.75%	14.4977	14.1219	10.6250
12.50%	14.3427	13.9719	10.4167
12.25%	14.1883	13.8226	10.2083
12.00%	14.0346	13.6742	10.0000
11.75%	13.8816	13.5266	9.7917
11.50%	13.7293	13.3797	9.5833
11.25%	13.5777	13.2337	9.3750
11.00%	13.4268	13.0884	9.1667
10.75%	13.2765	12.9440	8.9583
10.50%	13.1271	12.8004	8.7500
10.25%	12.9783	12.6576	8.5417
10.00%	12.8303	12.5157	8.3333
9.75%	12.6830	12.3746	8.1250
9.50%	12.5364	12.2343	7.9167
9.25%	12.3906	12.0949	7.7083
9.00%	12.2456	11.9563	7.5000
8.75%	12.1013	11.8186	7.2917
8.50%	11.9577	11.6818	7.0833
8.25%	11.8150	11.5458	6.8750
8.00%	11.6730	11.4107	6.6667
7.75%	11.5318	11.2765	6.4583
7.50%	11.3915	11.1431	6.2500
7.25%	11.2519	11.0106	6.0417
7.00%	11.1131	10.8791	5.8333

Term remaining: 11 years continued

Interest Rate	Repayment Mortgage Cost-per-£1,000		Interest-only Mortgage
	Annual Rest	Monthly/Daily Rest	Cost-per-£1,000
6.75%	10.9751	10.7484	5.6250
6.50%	10.8379	10.6186	5.4167
6.25%	10.7016	10.4897	5.2083
6.00%	10.5661	10.3617	5.0000
5.75%	10.4314	10.2346	4.7917
5.50%	10.2976	10.1084	4.5833
5.25%	10.1646	9.9831	4.3750
5.00%	10.0324	9.8588	4.1667
4.75%	9.9011	9.7354	3.9583
4.50%	9.7707	9.6129	3.7500
4.25%	9.6411	9.4913	3.5417
4.00%	9.5124	9.3706	3.3333
3.75%	9.3846	9.2509	3.1250
3.50%	9.2577	9.1321	2.9167
3.25%	9.1316	9.0143	2.7083
3.00%	9.0065	8.8974	2.5000
2.75%	8.8822	8.7814	2.2917
2.50%	8.7588	8.6664	2.0833
2.25%	8.6364	8.5523	1.8750
2.00%	8.5148	8.4391	1.6667
1.00%	8.0378	7.9960	0.8333

Term remaining: 12 years

Interest Rate	Repayment Mortgage Cost-per-£1,000		Interest-only Mortgage Cost-per-£1,000
	Annual Rest	Monthly/Daily Rest	
15.00%	15.3734	15.0063	12.5000
14.75%	15.2097	14.8457	12.2917
14.50%	15.0466	14.6859	12.0833
14.25%	14.8842	14.5268	11.8750
14.00%	14.7224	14.3686	11.6667
13.75%	14.5614	14.2111	11.4583
13.50%	14.4009	14.0544	11.2500
13.25%	14.2412	13.8985	11.0417
13.00%	14.0822	13.7433	10.8333
12.75%	13.9238	13.5890	10.6250
12.50%	13.7662	13.4356	10.4167
12.25%	13.6093	13.2829	10.2083
12.00%	13.4531	13.1311	10.0000
11.75%	13.2976	12.9801	9.7917
11.50%	13.1429	12.8299	9.5833
11.25%	12.9889	12.6806	9.3750
11.00%	12.8356	12.5322	9.1667
10.75%	12.6831	12.3846	8.9583
10.50%	12.5314	12.2379	8.7500
10.25%	12.3804	12.0921	8.5417
10.00%	12.2303	11.9472	8.3333
9.75%	12.0809	11.8031	8.1250
9.50%	11.9323	11.6600	7.9167
9.25%	11.7845	11.5178	7.7083
9.00%	11.6376	11.3764	7.5000
8.75%	11.4914	11.2360	7.2917
8.50%	11.3461	11.0965	7.0833
8.25%	11.2016	10.9580	6.8750
8.00%	11.0579	10.8204	6.6667
7.75%	10.9151	10.6837	6.4583
7.50%	10.7732	10.5480	6.2500
7.25%	10.6321	10.4132	6.0417
7.00%	10.4918	10.2794	5.8333

Term remaining: 12 years continued

Interest Rate	Repayment Mortgage Cost-per-£1,000		Interest-only Mortgage Cost-per-£1,000
	Annual Rest	Monthly/Daily Rest	
6.75%	10.3525	10.1465	5.6250
6.50%	10.2140	10.0146	5.4167
6.25%	10.0764	9.8837	5.2083
6.00%	9.9398	9.7537	5.0000
5.75%	9.8040	9.6248	4.7917
5.50%	9.6691	9.4968	4.5833
5.25%	9.5351	9.3698	4.3750
5.00%	9.4021	9.2438	4.1667
4.75%	9.2700	9.1188	3.9583
4.50%	9.1388	8.9948	3.7500
4.25%	9.0086	8.8718	3.5417
4.00%	8.8793	8.7499	3.3333
3.75%	8.7510	8.6289	3.1250
3.50%	8.6237	8.5089	2.9167
3.25%	8.4973	8.3900	2.7083
3.00%	8.3718	8.2721	2.5000
2.75%	8.2474	8.1552	2.2917
2.50%	8.1239	8.0393	2.0833
2.25%	8.0015	7.9245	1.8750
2.00%	7.8800	7.8107	1.6667
1.00%	7.4041	7.3658	0.8333

Term remaining: 13 years

Interest Rate	Repayment Mortgage Cost-per-£1,000		Interest-only Mortgage Cost-per-£1,000
	Annual Rest	Monthly/Daily Rest	
15.00%	14.9259	14.6008	12.5000
14.75%	14.7593	14.4366	12.2917
14.50%	14.5934	14.2732	12.0833
14.25%	14.4282	14.1106	11.8750
14.00%	14.2636	13.9487	11.6667
13.75%	14.0998	13.7877	11.4583
13.50%	13.9367	13.6275	11.2500
13.25%	13.7742	13.4682	11.0417
13.00%	13.6125	13.3096	10.8333
12.75%	13.4516	13.1519	10.6250
12.50%	13.2913	12.9951	10.4167
12.25%	13.1318	12.8391	10.2083
12.00%	12.9731	12.6840	10.0000
11.75%	12.8151	12.5297	9.7917
11.50%	12.6579	12.3764	9.5833
11.25%	12.5015	12.2239	9.3750
11.00%	12.3459	12.0724	9.1667
10.75%	12.1911	11.9217	8.9583
10.50%	12.0371	11.7720	8.7500
10.25%	11.8839	11.6232	8.5417
10.00%	11.7315	11.4753	8.3333
9.75%	11.5800	11.3284	8.1250
9.50%	11.4293	11.1825	7.9167
9.25%	11.2795	11.0374	7.7083
9.00%	11.1305	10.8934	7.5000
8.75%	10.9825	10.7503	7.2917
8.50%	10.8352	10.6083	7.0833
8.25%	10.6889	10.4672	6.8750
8.00%	10.5435	10.3271	6.6667
7.75%	10.3990	10.1880	6.4583
7.50%	10.2553	10.0499	6.2500
7.25%	10.1127	9.9128	6.0417
7.00%	9.9709	9.7768	5.8333

Term remaining: 13 years continued

Interest Rate	Repayment Mortgage Cost-per-£1,000		Interest-only Mortgage Cost-per-£1,000
	Annual Rest	**Monthly/Daily Rest**	
6.75%	9.8301	9.6418	5.6250
6.50%	9.6902	9.5078	5.4167
6.25%	9.5513	9.3749	5.2083
6.00%	9.4133	9.2430	5.0000
5.75%	9.2764	9.1122	4.7917
5.50%	9.1404	8.9824	4.5833
5.25%	9.0053	8.8537	4.3750
5.00%	8.8713	8.7260	4.1667
4.75%	8.7383	8.5995	3.9583
4.50%	8.6063	8.4740	3.7500
4.25%	8.4753	8.3496	3.5417
4.00%	8.3453	8.2263	3.3333
3.75%	8.2164	8.1040	3.1250
3.50%	8.0885	7.9829	2.9167
3.25%	7.9616	7.8629	2.7083
3.00%	7.8358	7.7440	2.5000
2.75%	7.7110	7.6261	2.2917
2.50%	7.5874	7.5094	2.0833
2.25%	7.4647	7.3938	1.8750
2.00%	7.3432	7.2794	1.6667
1.00%	6.8679	6.8326	0.8333

Term remaining: 14 years

Interest Rate	Repayment Mortgage Cost-per-£1,000		Interest-only Mortgage Cost-per-£1,000
	Annual Rest	Monthly/Daily Rest	
15.00%	14.5574	14.2686	12.5000
14.75%	14.3880	14.1010	12.2917
14.50%	14.2193	13.9342	12.0833
14.25%	14.0514	13.7682	11.8750
14.00%	13.8841	13.6030	11.6667
13.75%	13.7175	13.4386	11.4583
13.50%	13.5517	13.2750	11.2500
13.25%	13.3866	13.1123	11.0417
13.00%	13.2223	12.9505	10.8333
12.75%	13.0587	12.7896	10.6250
12.50%	12.8959	12.6295	10.4167
12.25%	12.7339	12.4703	10.2083
12.00%	12.5726	12.3120	10.0000
11.75%	12.4122	12.1546	9.7917
11.50%	12.2525	11.9981	9.5833
11.25%	12.0937	11.8426	9.3750
11.00%	11.9357	11.6880	9.1667
10.75%	11.7785	11.5344	8.9583
10.50%	11.6222	11.3817	8.7500
10.25%	11.4668	11.2300	8.5417
10.00%	11.3122	11.0793	8.3333
9.75%	11.1585	10.9295	8.1250
9.50%	11.0057	10.7808	7.9167
9.25%	10.8538	10.6331	7.7083
9.00%	10.7028	10.4864	7.5000
8.75%	10.5527	10.3407	7.2917
8.50%	10.4035	10.1961	7.0833
8.25%	10.2553	10.0525	6.8750
8.00%	10.1081	9.9099	6.6667
7.75%	9.9618	9.7685	6.4583
7.50%	9.8164	9.6281	6.2500
7.25%	9.6721	9.4887	6.0417
7.00%	9.5287	9.3505	5.8333

Term remaining: 14 years continued

Interest Rate	Repayment Mortgage Cost-per-£1,000		Interest-only Mortgage
	Annual Rest	Monthly/Daily Rest	Cost-per-£1,000
6.75%	9.3864	9.2133	5.6250
6.50%	9.2450	9.0773	5.4167
6.25%	9.1047	8.9424	5.2083
6.00%	8.9654	8.8085	5.0000
5.75%	8.8271	8.6759	4.7917
5.50%	8.6899	8.5443	4.5833
5.25%	8.5538	8.4139	4.3750
5.00%	8.4187	8.2846	4.1667
4.75%	8.2846	8.1565	3.9583
4.50%	8.1517	8.0295	3.7500
4.25%	8.0198	7.9037	3.5417
4.00%	7.8891	7.7790	3.3333
3.75%	7.7594	7.6555	3.1250
3.50%	7.6309	7.5332	2.9167
3.25%	7.5035	7.4121	2.7083
3.00%	7.3772	7.2922	2.5000
2.75%	7.2520	7.1734	2.2917
2.50%	7.1280	7.0558	2.0833
2.25%	7.0052	6.9395	1.8750
2.00%	6.8835	6.8243	1.6667
1.00%	6.4084	6.3757	0.8333

Term remaining: 15 years

Interest Rate	Repayment Mortgage Cost-per-£1,000		Interest-only Mortgage Cost-per-£1,000
	Annual Rest	Monthly/Daily Rest	
15.00%	14.2514	13.9944	12.5000
14.75%	14.0794	13.8235	12.2917
14.50%	13.9080	13.6534	12.0833
14.25%	13.7373	13.4842	11.8750
14.00%	13.5674	13.3158	11.6667
13.75%	13.3982	13.1482	11.4583
13.50%	13.2298	12.9815	11.2500
13.25%	13.0621	12.8156	11.0417
13.00%	12.8951	12.6506	10.8333
12.75%	12.7290	12.4865	10.6250
12.50%	12.5636	12.3233	10.4167
12.25%	12.3991	12.1610	10.2083
12.00%	12.2354	11.9997	10.0000
11.75%	12.0724	11.8393	9.7917
11.50%	11.9104	11.6798	9.5833
11.25%	11.7491	11.5213	9.3750
11.00%	11.5888	11.3638	9.1667
10.75%	11.4293	11.2072	8.9583
10.50%	11.2707	11.0517	8.7500
10.25%	11.1130	10.8972	8.5417
10.00%	10.9561	10.7436	8.3333
9.75%	10.8003	10.5912	8.1250
9.50%	10.6453	10.4397	7.9167
9.25%	10.4913	10.2893	7.7083
9.00%	10.3382	10.1400	7.5000
8.75%	10.1862	9.9918	7.2917
8.50%	10.0350	9.8446	7.0833
8.25%	9.8849	9.6986	6.8750
8.00%	9.7358	9.5536	6.6667
7.75%	9.5877	9.4098	6.4583
7.50%	9.4406	9.2671	6.2500
7.25%	9.2946	9.1255	6.0417
7.00%	9.1496	8.9851	5.8333

Term remaining: 15 years continued

Interest Rate	Repayment Mortgage Cost-per-£1,000		Interest-only Mortgage Cost-per-£1,000
	Annual Rest	Monthly/Daily Rest	
6.75%	9.0056	8.8459	5.6250
6.50%	8.8627	8.7078	5.4167
6.25%	8.7209	8.5709	5.2083
6.00%	8.5802	8.4351	5.0000
5.75%	8.4406	8.3006	4.7917
5.50%	8.3021	8.1672	4.5833
5.25%	8.1648	8.0351	4.3750
5.00%	8.0285	7.9042	4.1667
4.75%	7.8934	7.7745	3.9583
4.50%	7.7595	7.6460	3.7500
4.25%	7.6267	7.5188	3.5417
4.00%	7.4951	7.3928	3.3333
3.75%	7.3647	7.2681	3.1250
3.50%	7.2354	7.1446	2.9167
3.25%	7.1074	7.0224	2.7083
3.00%	6.9805	6.9014	2.5000
2.75%	6.8549	6.7817	2.2917
2.50%	6.7305	6.6633	2.0833
2.25%	6.6074	6.5462	1.8750
2.00%	6.4855	6.4303	1.6667
1.00%	6.0103	5.9798	0.8333

Term remaining: 16 years

Interest Rate	Repayment Mortgage Cost-per-£1,000		Interest-only Mortgage Cost-per-£1,000
	Annual Rest	Monthly/Daily Rest	
15.00%	13.9956	13.7664	12.5000
14.75%	13.8210	13.5925	12.2917
14.50%	13.6470	13.4194	12.0833
14.25%	13.4738	13.2471	11.8750
14.00%	13.3013	13.0756	11.6667
13.75%	13.1295	12.9050	11.4583
13.50%	12.9585	12.7352	11.2500
13.25%	12.7883	12.5663	11.0417
13.00%	12.6189	12.3983	10.8333
12.75%	12.4502	12.2312	10.6250
12.50%	12.2824	12.0650	10.4167
12.25%	12.1153	11.8998	10.2083
12.00%	11.9492	11.7355	10.0000
11.75%	11.7838	11.5722	9.7917
11.50%	11.6194	11.4098	9.5833
11.25%	11.4558	11.2485	9.3750
11.00%	11.2931	11.0881	9.1667
10.75%	11.1313	10.9287	8.9583
10.50%	10.9704	10.7704	8.7500
10.25%	10.8104	10.6131	8.5417
10.00%	10.6514	10.4569	8.3333
9.75%	10.4933	10.3017	8.1250
9.50%	10.3362	10.1477	7.9167
9.25%	10.1801	9.9947	7.7083
9.00%	10.0250	9.8428	7.5000
8.75%	9.8709	9.6921	7.2917
8.50%	9.7178	9.5424	7.0833
8.25%	9.5657	9.3940	6.8750
8.00%	9.4147	9.2467	6.6667
7.75%	9.2648	9.1005	6.4583
7.50%	9.1159	8.9556	6.2500
7.25%	8.9681	8.8118	6.0417
7.00%	8.8215	8.6692	5.8333

Term remaining: 16 years continued

Interest Rate	Repayment Mortgage Cost-per-£1,000		Interest-only Mortgage Cost-per-£1,000
	Annual Rest	Monthly/Daily Rest	
6.75%	8.6759	8.5279	5.6250
6.50%	8.5315	8.3878	5.4167
6.25%	8.3882	8.2489	5.2083
6.00%	8.2460	8.1113	5.0000
5.75%	8.1050	7.9749	4.7917
5.50%	7.9652	7.8398	4.5833
5.25%	7.8266	7.7059	4.3750
5.00%	7.6892	7.5734	4.1667
4.75%	7.5529	7.4421	3.9583
4.50%	7.4179	7.3122	3.7500
4.25%	7.2842	7.1836	3.5417
4.00%	7.1517	7.0562	3.3333
3.75%	7.0204	6.9302	3.1250
3.50%	6.8904	6.8056	2.9167
3.25%	6.7617	6.6823	2.7083
3.00%	6.6342	6.5603	2.5000
2.75%	6.5081	6.4396	2.2917
2.50%	6.3832	6.3204	2.0833
2.25%	6.2597	6.2025	1.8750
2.00%	6.1375	6.0859	1.6667
1.00%	5.6620	5.6335	0.8333

Term remaining: 17 years

Interest Rate	Repayment Mortgage Cost-per-£1,000		Interest-only Mortgage
	Annual Rest	Monthly/Daily Rest	Cost-per-£1,000
15.00%	13.7806	13.5759	12.5000
14.75%	13.6034	13.3991	12.2917
14.50%	13.4270	13.2231	12.0833
14.25%	13.2513	13.0479	11.8750
14.00%	13.0763	12.8736	11.6667
13.75%	12.9021	12.7000	11.4583
13.50%	12.7286	12.5274	11.2500
13.25%	12.5559	12.3557	11.0417
13.00%	12.3840	12.1848	10.8333
12.75%	12.2130	12.0148	10.6250
12.50%	12.0427	11.8458	10.4167
12.25%	11.8733	11.6778	10.2083
12.00%	11.7047	11.5106	10.0000
11.75%	11.5370	11.3445	9.7917
11.50%	11.3702	11.1794	9.5833
11.25%	11.2043	11.0152	9.3750
11.00%	11.0393	10.8521	9.1667
10.75%	10.8752	10.6900	8.9583
10.50%	10.7121	10.5290	8.7500
10.25%	10.5499	10.3691	8.5417
10.00%	10.3887	10.2102	8.3333
9.75%	10.2285	10.0525	8.1250
9.50%	10.0692	9.8958	7.9167
9.25%	9.9110	9.7403	7.7083
9.00%	9.7539	9.5860	7.5000
8.75%	9.5977	9.4327	7.2917
8.50%	9.4427	9.2807	7.0833
8.25%	9.2887	9.1299	6.8750
8.00%	9.1358	8.9803	6.6667
7.75%	8.9840	8.8318	6.4583
7.50%	8.8333	8.6847	6.2500
7.25%	8.6838	8.5387	6.0417
7.00%	8.5354	8.3940	5.8333

Term remaining: 17 years continued

Interest Rate	Repayment Mortgage Cost-per-£1,000 Annual Rest	Monthly/Daily Rest	Interest-only Mortgage Cost-per-£1,000
6.75%	8.3882	8.2506	5.6250
6.50%	8.2422	8.1085	5.4167
6.25%	8.0974	7.9677	5.2083
6.00%	7.9537	7.8282	5.0000
5.75%	7.8113	7.6900	4.7917
5.50%	7.6702	7.5531	4.5833
5.25%	7.5302	7.4176	4.3750
5.00%	7.3916	7.2834	4.1667
4.75%	7.2542	7.1506	3.9583
4.50%	7.1181	7.0192	3.7500
4.25%	6.9833	6.8892	3.5417
4.00%	6.8499	6.7605	3.3333
3.75%	6.7177	6.6333	3.1250
3.50%	6.5869	6.5074	2.9167
3.25%	6.4575	6.3830	2.7083
3.00%	6.3294	6.2600	2.5000
2.75%	6.2027	6.1384	2.2917
2.50%	6.0773	6.0183	2.0833
2.25%	5.9534	5.8996	1.8750
2.00%	5.8308	5.7824	1.6667
1.00%	5.3548	5.3280	0.8333

Term remaining: 18 years

Interest Rate	Repayment Mortgage Cost-per-£1,000		Interest-only Mortgage Cost-per-£1,000
	Annual Rest	Monthly/Daily Rest	
15.00%	13.5989	13.4160	12.5000
14.75%	13.4193	13.2365	12.2917
14.50%	13.2405	13.0578	12.0833
14.25%	13.0624	12.8799	11.8750
14.00%	12.8851	12.7028	11.6667
13.75%	12.7085	12.5266	11.4583
13.50%	12.5327	12.3512	11.2500
13.25%	12.3576	12.1767	11.0417
13.00%	12.1834	12.0032	10.8333
12.75%	12.0100	11.8305	10.6250
12.50%	11.8374	11.6588	10.4167
12.25%	11.6657	11.4880	10.2083
12.00%	11.4948	11.3182	10.0000
11.75%	11.3248	11.1494	9.7917
11.50%	11.1557	10.9816	9.5833
11.25%	10.9875	10.8148	9.3750
11.00%	10.8202	10.6490	9.1667
10.75%	10.6539	10.4843	8.9583
10.50%	10.4886	10.3207	8.7500
10.25%	10.3242	10.1582	8.5417
10.00%	10.1609	9.9968	8.3333
9.75%	9.9985	9.8365	8.1250
9.50%	9.8372	9.6774	7.9167
9.25%	9.6769	9.5194	7.7083
9.00%	9.5177	9.3626	7.5000
8.75%	9.3596	9.2070	7.2917
8.50%	9.2025	9.0526	7.0833
8.25%	9.0466	8.8995	6.8750
8.00%	8.8918	8.7475	6.6667
7.75%	8.7382	8.5969	6.4583
7.50%	8.5857	8.4475	6.2500
7.25%	8.4345	8.2995	6.0417
7.00%	8.2844	8.1527	5.8333

Term remaining: 18 years continued

Interest Rate	Repayment Mortgage Cost-per-£1,000		Interest-only Mortgage
	Annual Rest	Monthly/Daily Rest	Cost-per-£1,000
6.75%	8.1355	8.0073	5.6250
6.50%	7.9879	7.8632	5.4167
6.25%	7.8415	7.7204	5.2083
6.00%	7.6964	7.5790	5.0000
5.75%	7.5525	7.4390	4.7917
5.50%	7.4100	7.3004	4.5833
5.25%	7.2688	7.1632	4.3750
5.00%	7.1289	7.0275	4.1667
4.75%	6.9903	6.8931	3.9583
4.50%	6.8531	6.7602	3.7500
4.25%	6.7172	6.6288	3.5417
4.00%	6.5828	6.4988	3.3333
3.75%	6.4497	6.3703	3.1250
3.50%	6.3181	6.2433	2.9167
3.25%	6.1878	6.1178	2.7083
3.00%	6.0591	5.9937	2.5000
2.75%	5.9317	5.8712	2.2917
2.50%	5.8058	5.7502	2.0833
2.25%	5.6814	5.6308	1.8750
2.00%	5.5585	5.5128	1.6667
1.00%	5.0818	5.0565	0.8333

Term remaining: 19 years

Interest Rate	Repayment Mortgage Cost-per-£1,000		Interest-only Mortgage
	Annual Rest	Monthly/Daily Rest	Cost-per-£1,000
15.00%	13.4447	13.2812	12.5000
14.75%	13.2629	13.0992	12.2917
14.50%	13.0819	12.9179	12.0833
14.25%	12.9015	12.7375	11.8750
14.00%	12.7219	12.5579	11.6667
13.75%	12.5431	12.3791	11.4583
13.50%	12.3650	12.2012	11.2500
13.25%	12.1877	12.0241	11.0417
13.00%	12.0112	11.8480	10.8333
12.75%	11.8355	11.6727	10.6250
12.50%	11.6607	11.4984	10.4167
12.25%	11.4867	11.3251	10.2083
12.00%	11.3136	11.1527	10.0000
11.75%	11.1414	10.9813	9.7917
11.50%	10.9700	10.8110	9.5833
11.25%	10.7997	10.6416	9.3750
11.00%	10.6302	10.4733	9.1667
10.75%	10.4617	10.3061	8.9583
10.50%	10.2942	10.1400	8.7500
10.25%	10.1277	9.9750	8.5417
10.00%	9.9622	9.8111	8.3333
9.75%	9.7978	9.6484	8.1250
9.50%	9.6344	9.4868	7.9167
9.25%	9.4721	9.3265	7.7083
9.00%	9.3109	9.1673	7.5000
8.75%	9.1508	9.0094	7.2917
8.50%	8.9918	8.8527	7.0833
8.25%	8.8340	8.6973	6.8750
8.00%	8.6773	8.5431	6.6667
7.75%	8.5218	8.3903	6.4583
7.50%	8.3676	8.2388	6.2500
7.25%	8.2145	8.0886	6.0417
7.00%	8.0628	7.9398	5.8333

Term remaining: 19 years continued

Interest Rate	Repayment Mortgage Cost-per-£1,000		Interest-only Mortgage Cost-per-£1,000
	Annual Rest	Monthly/Daily Rest	
6.75%	7.9122	7.7924	5.6250
6.50%	7.7630	7.6463	5.4167
6.25%	7.6150	7.5017	5.2083
6.00%	7.4684	7.3585	5.0000
5.75%	7.3231	7.2167	4.7917
5.50%	7.1792	7.0764	4.5833
5.25%	7.0366	6.9375	4.3750
5.00%	6.8954	6.8001	4.1667
4.75%	6.7556	6.6643	3.9583
4.50%	6.6173	6.5299	3.7500
4.25%	6.4804	6.3971	3.5417
4.00%	6.3449	6.2658	3.3333
3.75%	6.2109	6.1360	3.1250
3.50%	6.0784	6.0078	2.9167
3.25%	5.9473	5.8812	2.7083
3.00%	5.8178	5.7562	2.5000
2.75%	5.6898	5.6327	2.2917
2.50%	5.5634	5.5108	2.0833
2.25%	5.4385	5.3906	1.8750
2.00%	5.3151	5.2720	1.6667
1.00%	4.8376	4.8137	0.8333

Term remaining: 20 years

Interest Rate	Repayment Mortgage Cost-per-£1,000		Interest-only Mortgage Cost-per-£1,000
	Annual Rest	Monthly/Daily Rest	
15.00%	13.3135	13.1672	12.5000
14.75%	13.1296	12.9829	12.2917
14.50%	12.9464	12.7993	12.0833
14.25%	12.7639	12.6164	11.8750
14.00%	12.5822	12.4344	11.6667
13.75%	12.4012	12.2533	11.4583
13.50%	12.2209	12.0729	11.2500
13.25%	12.0415	11.8935	11.0417
13.00%	11.8628	11.7149	10.8333
12.75%	11.6850	11.5372	10.6250
12.50%	11.5080	11.3605	10.4167
12.25%	11.3318	11.1847	10.2083
12.00%	11.1566	11.0099	10.0000
11.75%	10.9822	10.8360	9.7917
11.50%	10.8087	10.6632	9.5833
11.25%	10.6362	10.4914	9.3750
11.00%	10.4646	10.3207	9.1667
10.75%	10.2940	10.1511	8.9583
10.50%	10.1244	9.9826	8.7500
10.25%	9.9559	9.8152	8.5417
10.00%	9.7883	9.6489	8.3333
9.75%	9.6218	9.4838	8.1250
9.50%	9.4564	9.3199	7.9167
9.25%	9.2921	9.1572	7.7083
9.00%	9.1289	8.9958	7.5000
8.75%	8.9668	8.8356	7.2917
8.50%	8.8059	8.6766	7.0833
8.25%	8.6462	8.5190	6.8750
8.00%	8.4877	8.3627	6.6667
7.75%	8.3304	8.2077	6.4583
7.50%	8.1743	8.0541	6.2500
7.25%	8.0196	7.9019	6.0417
7.00%	7.8661	7.7511	5.8333

Term remaining: 20 years continued

Interest Rate	Repayment Mortgage Cost-per-£1,000		Interest-only Mortgage Cost-per-£1,000
	Annual Rest	Monthly/Daily Rest	
6.75%	7.7139	7.6017	5.6250
6.50%	7.5630	7.4537	5.4167
6.25%	7.4135	7.3072	5.2083
6.00%	7.2654	7.1621	5.0000
5.75%	7.1186	7.0186	4.7917
5.50%	6.9733	6.8766	4.5833
5.25%	6.8294	6.7361	4.3750
5.00%	6.6869	6.5971	4.1667
4.75%	6.5459	6.4597	3.9583
4.50%	6.4063	6.3239	3.7500
4.25%	6.2683	6.1897	3.5417
4.00%	6.1318	6.0571	3.3333
3.75%	5.9968	5.9261	3.1250
3.50%	5.8634	5.7967	2.9167
3.25%	5.7316	5.6690	2.7083
3.00%	5.6013	5.5429	2.5000
2.75%	5.4726	5.4185	2.2917
2.50%	5.3456	5.2958	2.0833
2.25%	5.2202	5.1748	1.8750
2.00%	5.0964	5.0554	1.6667
1.00%	4.6179	4.5952	0.8333

Term remaining: 21 years

Interest Rate	Repayment Mortgage Cost-per-£1,000		Interest-only Mortgage Cost-per-£1,000
	Annual Rest	Monthly/Daily Rest	
15.00%	13.2014	13.0706	12.5000
14.75%	13.0155	12.8841	12.2917
14.50%	12.8303	12.6983	12.0833
14.25%	12.6458	12.5132	11.8750
14.00%	12.4621	12.3290	11.6667
13.75%	12.2790	12.1456	11.4583
13.50%	12.0968	11.9630	11.2500
13.25%	11.9152	11.7812	11.0417
13.00%	11.7345	11.6004	10.8333
12.75%	11.5546	11.4204	10.6250
12.50%	11.3756	11.2414	10.4167
12.25%	11.1973	11.0632	10.2083
12.00%	11.0200	10.8861	10.0000
11.75%	10.8436	10.7100	9.7917
11.50%	10.6680	10.5348	9.5833
11.25%	10.4935	10.3607	9.3750
11.00%	10.3198	10.1877	9.1667
10.75%	10.1472	10.0157	8.9583
10.50%	9.9755	9.8449	8.7500
10.25%	9.8049	9.6752	8.5417
10.00%	9.6354	9.5066	8.3333
9.75%	9.4669	9.3393	8.1250
9.50%	9.2995	9.1731	7.9167
9.25%	9.1332	9.0081	7.7083
9.00%	8.9681	8.8445	7.5000
8.75%	8.8041	8.6821	7.2917
8.50%	8.6413	8.5210	7.0833
8.25%	8.4797	8.3612	6.8750
8.00%	8.3194	8.2027	6.6667
7.75%	8.1603	8.0457	6.4583
7.50%	8.0024	7.8900	6.2500
7.25%	7.8459	7.7358	6.0417
7.00%	7.6908	7.5830	5.8333

Term remaining: 21 years continued

Interest Rate	Repayment Mortgage Cost-per-£1,000		Interest-only Mortgage
	Annual Rest	Monthly/Daily Rest	Cost-per-£1,000
6.75%	7.5369	7.4316	5.6250
6.50%	7.3844	7.2818	5.4167
6.25%	7.2334	7.1334	5.2083
6.00%	7.0837	6.9866	5.0000
5.75%	6.9355	6.8413	4.7917
5.50%	6.7887	6.6976	4.5833
5.25%	6.6435	6.5555	4.3750
5.00%	6.4997	6.4149	4.1667
4.75%	6.3574	6.2760	3.9583
4.50%	6.2167	6.1388	3.7500
4.25%	6.0776	6.0032	3.5417
4.00%	5.9400	5.8693	3.3333
3.75%	5.8041	5.7370	3.1250
3.50%	5.6697	5.6065	2.9167
3.25%	5.5370	5.4777	2.7083
3.00%	5.4060	5.3506	2.5000
2.75%	5.2766	5.2253	2.2917
2.50%	5.1489	5.1017	2.0833
2.25%	5.0230	4.9799	1.8750
2.00%	4.8987	4.8598	1.6667
1.00%	4.4192	4.3976	0.8333

Term remaining: 22 years

Interest Rate	Repayment Mortgage Cost-per-£1,000 Annual Rest	Repayment Mortgage Cost-per-£1,000 Monthly/Daily Rest	Interest-only Mortgage Cost-per-£1,000
15.00%	13.1055	12.9885	12.5000
14.75%	12.9177	12.7999	12.2917
14.50%	12.7307	12.6121	12.0833
14.25%	12.5443	12.4250	11.8750
14.00%	12.3586	12.2387	11.6667
13.75%	12.1736	12.0532	11.4583
13.50%	11.9894	11.8685	11.2500
13.25%	11.8060	11.6846	11.0417
13.00%	11.6233	11.5016	10.8333
12.75%	11.4414	11.3195	10.6250
12.50%	11.2604	11.1382	10.4167
12.25%	11.0802	10.9579	10.2083
12.00%	10.9009	10.7786	10.0000
11.75%	10.7224	10.6002	9.7917
11.50%	10.5449	10.4229	9.5833
11.25%	10.3684	10.2466	9.3750
11.00%	10.1928	10.0713	9.1667
10.75%	10.0181	9.8972	8.9583
10.50%	9.8445	9.7241	8.7500
10.25%	9.6719	9.5522	8.5417
10.00%	9.5004	9.3814	8.3333
9.75%	9.3300	9.2118	8.1250
9.50%	9.1607	9.0435	7.9167
9.25%	8.9925	8.8764	7.7083
9.00%	8.8254	8.7105	7.5000
8.75%	8.6596	8.5460	7.2917
8.50%	8.4949	8.3828	7.0833
8.25%	8.3315	8.2209	6.8750
8.00%	8.1693	8.0604	6.6667
7.75%	8.0085	7.9013	6.4583
7.50%	7.8489	7.7436	6.2500
7.25%	7.6907	7.5874	6.0417
7.00%	7.5338	7.4326	5.8333

Term remaining: 22 years continued

Interest Rate	Repayment Mortgage Cost-per-£1,000		Interest-only Mortgage
	Annual Rest	**Monthly/Daily Rest**	**Cost-per-£1,000**
6.75%	7.3783	7.2794	5.6250
6.50%	7.2243	7.1277	5.4167
6.25%	7.0716	6.9775	5.2083
6.00%	6.9205	6.8289	5.0000
5.75%	6.7708	6.6819	4.7917
5.50%	6.6226	6.5365	4.5833
5.25%	6.4760	6.3928	4.3750
5.00%	6.3309	6.2507	4.1667
4.75%	6.1874	6.1103	3.9583
4.50%	6.0455	5.9716	3.7500
4.25%	5.9052	5.8347	3.5417
4.00%	5.7666	5.6994	3.3333
3.75%	5.6296	5.5660	3.1250
3.50%	5.4943	5.4343	2.9167
3.25%	5.3608	5.3044	2.7083
3.00%	5.2289	5.1763	2.5000
2.75%	5.0989	5.0500	2.2917
2.50%	4.9706	4.9256	2.0833
2.25%	4.8440	4.8030	1.8750
2.00%	4.7193	4.6822	1.6667
1.00%	4.2386	4.2180	0.8333

Term remaining: 23 years

Interest Rate	Repayment Mortgage Cost-per-£1,000		Interest-only Mortgage Cost-per-£1,000
	Annual Rest	Monthly/Daily Rest	
15.00%	13.0232	12.9186	12.5000
14.75%	12.8337	12.7282	12.2917
14.50%	12.6449	12.5385	12.0833
14.25%	12.4567	12.3495	11.8750
14.00%	12.2692	12.1612	11.6667
13.75%	12.0825	11.9738	11.4583
13.50%	11.8964	11.7871	11.2500
13.25%	11.7111	11.6012	11.0417
13.00%	11.5266	11.4162	10.8333
12.75%	11.3429	11.2320	10.6250
12.50%	11.1599	11.0487	10.4167
12.25%	10.9779	10.8664	10.2083
12.00%	10.7967	10.6850	10.0000
11.75%	10.6163	10.5045	9.7917
11.50%	10.4369	10.3251	9.5833
11.25%	10.2584	10.1466	9.3750
11.00%	10.0809	9.9693	9.1667
10.75%	9.9044	9.7930	8.9583
10.50%	9.7289	9.6178	8.7500
10.25%	9.5544	9.4438	8.5417
10.00%	9.3810	9.2709	8.3333
9.75%	9.2087	9.0992	8.1250
9.50%	9.0374	8.9287	7.9167
9.25%	8.8674	8.7595	7.7083
9.00%	8.6985	8.5916	7.5000
8.75%	8.5308	8.4250	7.2917
8.50%	8.3643	8.2597	7.0833
8.25%	8.1991	8.0958	6.8750
8.00%	8.0352	7.9333	6.6667
7.75%	7.8726	7.7722	6.4583
7.50%	7.7113	7.6125	6.2500
7.25%	7.5514	7.4544	6.0417
7.00%	7.3928	7.2977	5.8333

Term remaining: 23 years continued

Interest Rate	Repayment Mortgage Cost-per-£1,000		Interest-only Mortgage
	Annual Rest	Monthly/Daily Rest	Cost-per-£1,000
6.75%	7.2357	7.1426	5.6250
6.50%	7.0801	6.9891	5.4167
6.25%	6.9259	6.8371	5.2083
6.00%	6.7732	6.6868	5.0000
5.75%	6.6221	6.5381	4.7917
5.50%	6.4725	6.3911	4.5833
5.25%	6.3245	6.2457	4.3750
5.00%	6.1781	6.1021	4.1667
4.75%	6.0333	5.9602	3.9583
4.50%	5.8902	5.8201	3.7500
4.25%	5.7488	5.6818	3.5417
4.00%	5.6091	5.5453	3.3333
3.75%	5.4711	5.4106	3.1250
3.50%	5.3349	5.2777	2.9167
3.25%	5.2005	5.1468	2.7083
3.00%	5.0678	5.0176	2.5000
2.75%	4.9370	4.8904	2.2917
2.50%	4.8080	4.7651	2.0833
2.25%	4.6809	4.6417	1.8750
2.00%	4.5557	4.5203	1.6667
1.00%	4.0738	4.0541	0.8333

Term remaining: 24 years

Interest Rate	Repayment Mortgage Cost-per-£1,000		Interest-only Mortgage Cost-per-£1,000
	Annual Rest	Monthly/Daily Rest	
15.00%	12.9525	12.8589	12.5000
14.75%	12.7614	12.6668	12.2917
14.50%	12.5709	12.4754	12.0833
14.25%	12.3811	12.2846	11.8750
14.00%	12.1919	12.0946	11.6667
13.75%	12.0034	11.9053	11.4583
13.50%	11.8157	11.7168	11.2500
13.25%	11.6286	11.5291	11.0417
13.00%	11.4424	11.3422	10.8333
12.75%	11.2569	11.1561	10.6250
12.50%	11.0722	10.9709	10.4167
12.25%	10.8883	10.7866	10.2083
12.00%	10.7053	10.6032	10.0000
11.75%	10.5232	10.4208	9.7917
11.50%	10.3419	10.2394	9.5833
11.25%	10.1616	10.0589	9.3750
11.00%	9.9823	9.8796	9.1667
10.75%	9.8039	9.7012	8.9583
10.50%	9.6265	9.5240	8.7500
10.25%	9.4502	9.3480	8.5417
10.00%	9.2750	9.1730	8.3333
9.75%	9.1008	8.9993	8.1250
9.50%	8.9278	8.8268	7.9167
9.25%	8.7559	8.6556	7.7083
9.00%	8.5852	8.4857	7.5000
8.75%	8.4157	8.3170	7.2917
8.50%	8.2475	8.1498	7.0833
8.25%	8.0805	7.9839	6.8750
8.00%	7.9148	7.8194	6.6667
7.75%	7.7505	7.6564	6.4583
7.50%	7.5875	7.4948	6.2500
7.25%	7.4259	7.3348	6.0417
7.00%	7.2658	7.1763	5.8333

Term remaining: 24 years continued

Interest Rate	Repayment Mortgage Cost-per-£1,000		Interest-only Mortgage
	Annual Rest	Monthly/Daily Rest	Cost-per-£1,000
6.75%	7.1070	7.0193	5.6250
6.50%	6.9498	6.8640	5.4167
6.25%	6.7941	6.7103	5.2083
6.00%	6.6399	6.5582	5.0000
5.75%	6.4873	6.4079	4.7917
5.50%	6.3363	6.2592	4.5833
5.25%	6.1869	6.1123	4.3750
5.00%	6.0392	5.9672	4.1667
4.75%	5.8932	5.8238	3.9583
4.50%	5.7489	5.6823	3.7500
4.25%	5.6064	5.5426	3.5417
4.00%	5.4656	5.4048	3.3333
3.75%	5.3266	5.2689	3.1250
3.50%	5.1894	5.1349	2.9167
3.25%	5.0541	5.0028	2.7083
3.00%	4.9206	4.8727	2.5000
2.75%	4.7891	4.7446	2.2917
2.50%	4.6594	4.6184	2.0833
2.25%	4.5317	4.4942	1.8750
2.00%	4.4059	4.3721	1.6667
1.00%	3.9228	3.9039	0.8333

Term remaining: 25 years

Interest Rate	Repayment Mortgage Cost-per-£1,000		Interest-only Mortgage
	Annual Rest	Monthly/Daily Rest	Cost-per-£1,000
15.00%	12.8916	12.8080	12.5000
14.75%	12.6990	12.6143	12.2917
14.50%	12.5070	12.4213	12.0833
14.25%	12.3156	12.2289	11.8750
14.00%	12.1249	12.0372	11.6667
13.75%	11.9348	11.8463	11.4583
13.50%	11.7454	11.6560	11.2500
13.25%	11.5568	11.4666	11.0417
13.00%	11.3688	11.2779	10.8333
12.75%	11.1817	11.0901	10.6250
12.50%	10.9953	10.9031	10.4167
12.25%	10.8097	10.7169	10.2083
12.00%	10.6250	10.5317	10.0000
11.75%	10.4411	10.3474	9.7917
11.50%	10.2582	10.1641	9.5833
11.25%	10.0761	9.9818	9.3750
11.00%	9.8950	9.8005	9.1667
10.75%	9.7149	9.6203	8.9583
10.50%	9.5358	9.4411	8.7500
10.25%	9.3577	9.2631	8.5417
10.00%	9.1807	9.0863	8.3333
9.75%	9.0047	8.9106	8.1250
9.50%	8.8299	8.7361	7.9167
9.25%	8.6563	8.5630	7.7083
9.00%	8.4839	8.3911	7.5000
8.75%	8.3126	8.2205	7.2917
8.50%	8.1426	8.0513	7.0833
8.25%	7.9739	7.8835	6.8750
8.00%	7.8066	7.7171	6.6667
7.75%	7.6405	7.5522	6.4583
7.50%	7.4759	7.3888	6.2500
7.25%	7.3127	7.2269	6.0417
7.00%	7.1509	7.0666	5.8333

Term remaining: 25 years continued

Interest Rate	Repayment Mortgage Cost-per-£1,000		Interest-only Mortgage
	Annual Rest	Monthly/Daily Rest	Cost-per-£1,000
6.75%	6.9906	6.9078	5.6250
6.50%	6.8318	6.7507	5.4167
6.25%	6.6746	6.5953	5.2083
6.00%	6.5189	6.4416	5.0000
5.75%	6.3648	6.2896	4.7917
5.50%	6.2124	6.1393	4.5833
5.25%	6.0617	5.9909	4.3750
5.00%	5.9127	5.8442	4.1667
4.75%	5.7654	5.6994	3.9583
4.50%	5.6199	5.5565	3.7500
4.25%	5.4762	5.4155	3.5417
4.00%	5.3343	5.2764	3.3333
3.75%	5.1943	5.1393	3.1250
3.50%	5.0562	5.0041	2.9167
3.25%	4.9199	4.8710	2.7083
3.00%	4.7857	4.7399	2.5000
2.75%	4.6533	4.6108	2.2917
2.50%	4.5230	4.4838	2.0833
2.25%	4.3947	4.3588	1.8750
2.00%	4.2684	4.2360	1.6667
1.00%	3.7839	3.7658	0.8333

Term remaining: 26 years

Interest Rate	Repayment Mortgage Cost-per-£1,000 Annual Rest	Repayment Mortgage Cost-per-£1,000 Monthly/Daily Rest	Interest-only Mortgage Cost-per-£1,000
15.00%	12.8392	12.7644	12.5000
14.75%	12.6451	12.5693	12.2917
14.50%	12.4517	12.3748	12.0833
14.25%	12.2589	12.1810	11.8750
14.00%	12.0667	11.9878	11.6667
13.75%	11.8751	11.7952	11.4583
13.50%	11.6842	11.6034	11.2500
13.25%	11.4940	11.4124	11.0417
13.00%	11.3045	11.2220	10.8333
12.75%	11.1158	11.0325	10.6250
12.50%	10.9278	10.8438	10.4167
12.25%	10.7407	10.6560	10.2083
12.00%	10.5543	10.4691	10.0000
11.75%	10.3688	10.2830	9.7917
11.50%	10.1842	10.0979	9.5833
11.25%	10.0005	9.9138	9.3750
11.00%	9.8177	9.7307	9.1667
10.75%	9.6359	9.5487	8.9583
10.50%	9.4551	9.3677	8.7500
10.25%	9.2753	9.1878	8.5417
10.00%	9.0966	9.0091	8.3333
9.75%	8.9190	8.8316	8.1250
9.50%	8.7424	8.6552	7.9167
9.25%	8.5671	8.4802	7.7083
9.00%	8.3929	8.3064	7.5000
8.75%	8.2200	8.1340	7.2917
8.50%	8.0483	7.9629	7.0833
8.25%	7.8780	7.7933	6.8750
8.00%	7.7089	7.6250	6.6667
7.75%	7.5412	7.4583	6.4583
7.50%	7.3750	7.2930	6.2500
7.25%	7.2101	7.1293	6.0417
7.00%	7.0468	6.9672	5.8333

Term remaining: 26 years continued

Interest Rate	Repayment Mortgage Cost-per-£1,000		Interest-only Mortgage
	Annual Rest	Monthly/Daily Rest	Cost-per-£1,000
6.75%	6.8849	6.8068	5.6250
6.50%	6.7246	6.6479	5.4167
6.25%	6.5658	6.4908	5.2083
6.00%	6.4087	6.3354	5.0000
5.75%	6.2532	6.1818	4.7917
5.50%	6.0994	6.0300	4.5833
5.25%	5.9473	5.8800	4.3750
5.00%	5.7970	5.7319	4.1667
4.75%	5.6485	5.5856	3.9583
4.50%	5.5018	5.4413	3.7500
4.25%	5.3569	5.2990	3.5417
4.00%	5.2139	5.1587	3.3333
3.75%	5.0729	5.0203	3.1250
3.50%	4.9338	4.8840	2.9167
3.25%	4.7967	4.7498	2.7083
3.00%	4.6615	4.6177	2.5000
2.75%	4.5284	4.4877	2.2917
2.50%	4.3974	4.3598	2.0833
2.25%	4.2684	4.2341	1.8750
2.00%	4.1416	4.1105	1.6667
1.00%	3.6557	3.6384	0.8333

Term remaining: 27 years

Interest Rate	Repayment Mortgage Cost-per-£1,000		Interest-only Mortgage Cost-per-£1,000
	Annual Rest	Monthly/Daily Rest	
15.00%	12.7939	12.7272	12.5000
14.75%	12.5986	12.5307	12.2917
14.50%	12.4038	12.3349	12.0833
14.25%	12.2096	12.1397	11.8750
14.00%	12.0161	11.9450	11.6667
13.75%	11.8231	11.7511	11.4583
13.50%	11.6308	11.5578	11.2500
13.25%	11.4392	11.3652	11.0417
13.00%	11.2483	11.1734	10.8333
12.75%	11.0580	10.9824	10.6250
12.50%	10.8686	10.7921	10.4167
12.25%	10.6799	10.6027	10.2083
12.00%	10.4920	10.4141	10.0000
11.75%	10.3050	10.2264	9.7917
11.50%	10.1188	10.0396	9.5833
11.25%	9.9335	9.8538	9.3750
11.00%	9.7491	9.6690	9.1667
10.75%	9.5657	9.4852	8.9583
10.50%	9.3832	9.3025	8.7500
10.25%	9.2018	9.1209	8.5417
10.00%	9.0215	8.9404	8.3333
9.75%	8.8422	8.7611	8.1250
9.50%	8.6640	8.5829	7.9167
9.25%	8.4870	8.4061	7.7083
9.00%	8.3112	8.2305	7.5000
8.75%	8.1367	8.0563	7.2917
8.50%	7.9634	7.8834	7.0833
8.25%	7.7913	7.7119	6.8750
8.00%	7.6207	7.5419	6.6667
7.75%	7.4514	7.3734	6.4583
7.50%	7.2835	7.2064	6.2500
7.25%	7.1171	7.0409	6.0417
7.00%	6.9521	6.8771	5.8333

Term remaining: 27 years continued

Interest Rate	Repayment Mortgage Cost-per-£1,000		Interest-only Mortgage
	Annual Rest	Monthly/Daily Rest	Cost-per-£1,000
6.75%	6.7887	6.7149	5.6250
6.50%	6.6269	6.5544	5.4167
6.25%	6.4667	6.3956	5.2083
6.00%	6.3081	6.2386	5.0000
5.75%	6.1512	6.0834	4.7917
5.50%	5.9960	5.9300	4.5833
5.25%	5.8426	5.7785	4.3750
5.00%	5.6910	5.6289	4.1667
4.75%	5.5412	5.4813	3.9583
4.50%	5.3933	5.3356	3.7500
4.25%	5.2473	5.1920	3.5417
4.00%	5.1032	5.0504	3.3333
3.75%	4.9611	4.9108	3.1250
3.50%	4.8210	4.7734	2.9167
3.25%	4.6830	4.6381	2.7083
3.00%	4.5470	4.5050	2.5000
2.75%	4.4131	4.3741	2.2917
2.50%	4.2814	4.2453	2.0833
2.25%	4.1518	4.1188	1.8750
2.00%	4.0244	3.9946	1.6667
1.00%	3.5371	3.5204	0.8333

Term remaining: 28 years

Interest Rate	Repayment Mortgage Cost-per-£1,000		Interest-only Mortgage Cost-per-£1,000
	Annual Rest	Monthly/Daily Rest	
15.00%	12.7548	12.6952	12.5000
14.75%	12.5583	12.4976	12.2917
14.50%	12.3623	12.3005	12.0833
14.25%	12.1669	12.1040	11.8750
14.00%	11.9720	11.9081	11.6667
13.75%	11.7778	11.7128	11.4583
13.50%	11.5842	11.5182	11.2500
13.25%	11.3912	11.3243	11.0417
13.00%	11.1989	11.1310	10.8333
12.75%	11.0073	10.9385	10.6250
12.50%	10.8164	10.7468	10.4167
12.25%	10.6263	10.5559	10.2083
12.00%	10.4370	10.3658	10.0000
11.75%	10.2485	10.1765	9.7917
11.50%	10.0608	9.9882	9.5833
11.25%	9.8740	9.8008	9.3750
11.00%	9.6881	9.6144	9.1667
10.75%	9.5031	9.4289	8.9583
10.50%	9.3192	9.2445	8.7500
10.25%	9.1362	9.0612	8.5417
10.00%	8.9543	8.8791	8.3333
9.75%	8.7734	8.6980	8.1250
9.50%	8.5937	8.5182	7.9167
9.25%	8.4151	8.3396	7.7083
9.00%	8.2377	8.1623	7.5000
8.75%	8.0615	7.9864	7.2917
8.50%	7.8866	7.8117	7.0833
8.25%	7.7130	7.6385	6.8750
8.00%	7.5407	7.4668	6.6667
7.75%	7.3699	7.2965	6.4583
7.50%	7.2004	7.1278	6.2500
7.25%	7.0325	6.9606	6.0417
7.00%	6.8660	6.7951	5.8333

Term remaining: 28 years continued

Interest Rate	Repayment Mortgage Cost-per-£1,000		Interest-only Mortgage
	Annual Rest	Monthly/Daily Rest	Cost-per-£1,000
6.75%	6.7011	6.6313	5.6250
6.50%	6.5378	6.4691	5.4167
6.25%	6.3761	6.3087	5.2083
6.00%	6.2160	6.1501	5.0000
5.75%	6.0577	5.9933	4.7917
5.50%	5.9012	5.8384	4.5833
5.25%	5.7465	5.6854	4.3750
5.00%	5.5935	5.5344	4.1667
4.75%	5.4425	5.3853	3.9583
4.50%	5.2934	5.2383	3.7500
4.25%	5.1462	5.0934	3.5417
4.00%	5.0011	4.9505	3.3333
3.75%	4.8580	4.8098	3.1250
3.50%	4.7169	4.6712	2.9167
3.25%	4.5779	4.5349	2.7083
3.00%	4.4411	4.4008	2.5000
2.75%	4.3064	4.2689	2.2917
2.50%	4.1740	4.1393	2.0833
2.25%	4.0438	4.0120	1.8750
2.00%	3.9158	3.8871	1.6667
1.00%	3.4270	3.4109	0.8333

Term remaining: 29 years

Interest Rate	Repayment Mortgage Cost-per-£1,000		Interest-only Mortgage Cost-per-£1,000
	Annual Rest	Monthly/Daily Rest	
15.00%	12.7209	12.6678	12.5000
14.75%	12.5233	12.4691	12.2917
14.50%	12.3263	12.2709	12.0833
14.25%	12.1297	12.0733	11.8750
14.00%	11.9337	11.8762	11.6667
13.75%	11.7382	11.6797	11.4583
13.50%	11.5434	11.4838	11.2500
13.25%	11.3492	11.2886	11.0417
13.00%	11.1556	11.0941	10.8333
12.75%	10.9627	10.9002	10.6250
12.50%	10.7705	10.7071	10.4167
12.25%	10.5791	10.5148	10.2083
12.00%	10.3884	10.3233	10.0000
11.75%	10.1984	10.1326	9.7917
11.50%	10.0094	9.9428	9.5833
11.25%	9.8211	9.7539	9.3750
11.00%	9.6338	9.5659	9.1667
10.75%	9.4474	9.3789	8.9583
10.50%	9.2619	9.1930	8.7500
10.25%	9.0774	9.0081	8.5417
10.00%	8.8940	8.8243	8.3333
9.75%	8.7116	8.6416	8.1250
9.50%	8.5304	8.4602	7.9167
9.25%	8.3502	8.2799	7.7083
9.00%	8.1713	8.1010	7.5000
8.75%	7.9936	7.9233	7.2917
8.50%	7.8171	7.7470	7.0833
8.25%	7.6420	7.5722	6.8750
8.00%	7.4682	7.3987	6.6667
7.75%	7.2958	7.2268	6.4583
7.50%	7.1248	7.0564	6.2500
7.25%	6.9554	6.8876	6.0417
7.00%	6.7874	6.7204	5.8333

Term remaining: 29 years continued

Interest Rate	Repayment Mortgage Cost-per-£1,000		Interest-only Mortgage Cost-per-£1,000
	Annual Rest	**Monthly/Daily Rest**	
6.75%	6.6210	6.5549	5.6250
6.50%	6.4562	6.3912	5.4167
6.25%	6.2931	6.2292	5.2083
6.00%	6.1316	6.0690	5.0000
5.75%	5.9719	5.9107	4.7917
5.50%	5.8140	5.7542	4.5833
5.25%	5.6580	5.5998	4.3750
5.00%	5.5038	5.4473	4.1667
4.75%	5.3515	5.2969	3.9583
4.50%	5.2012	5.1485	3.7500
4.25%	5.0529	5.0023	3.5417
4.00%	4.9067	4.8582	3.3333
3.75%	4.7625	4.7163	3.1250
3.50%	4.6204	4.5766	2.9167
3.25%	4.4806	4.4392	2.7083
3.00%	4.3429	4.3041	2.5000
2.75%	4.2074	4.1713	2.2917
2.50%	4.0743	4.0409	2.0833
2.25%	3.9434	3.9129	1.8750
2.00%	3.8149	3.7872	1.6667
1.00%	3.3246	3.3091	0.8333

Term remaining: 30 years

Interest Rate	Repayment Mortgage Cost-per-£1,000		Interest-only Mortgage
	Annual Rest	Monthly/Daily Rest	Cost-per-£1,000
15.00%	12.6917	12.6443	12.5000
14.75%	12.4931	12.4446	12.2917
14.50%	12.2950	12.2454	12.0833
14.25%	12.0973	12.0467	11.8750
14.00%	11.9002	11.8485	11.6667
13.75%	11.7037	11.6509	11.4583
13.50%	11.5077	11.4539	11.2500
13.25%	11.3123	11.2575	11.0417
13.00%	11.1176	11.0618	10.8333
12.75%	10.9234	10.8667	10.6250
12.50%	10.7300	10.6723	10.4167
12.25%	10.5373	10.4787	10.2083
12.00%	10.3453	10.2858	10.0000
11.75%	10.1541	10.0938	9.7917
11.50%	9.9637	9.9026	9.5833
11.25%	9.7741	9.7123	9.3750
11.00%	9.5854	9.5229	9.1667
10.75%	9.3976	9.3344	8.9583
10.50%	9.2107	9.1470	8.7500
10.25%	9.0248	8.9606	8.5417
10.00%	8.8399	8.7753	8.3333
9.75%	8.6561	8.5911	8.1250
9.50%	8.4734	8.4081	7.9167
9.25%	8.2918	8.2262	7.7083
9.00%	8.1114	8.0457	7.5000
8.75%	7.9322	7.8664	7.2917
8.50%	7.7542	7.6885	7.0833
8.25%	7.5776	7.5120	6.8750
8.00%	7.4023	7.3370	6.6667
7.75%	7.2284	7.1634	6.4583
7.50%	7.0559	6.9914	6.2500
7.25%	6.8850	6.8210	6.0417
7.00%	6.7155	6.6522	5.8333

Term remaining: 30 years continued

Interest Rate	Repayment Mortgage Cost-per-£1,000		Interest-only Mortgage
	Annual Rest	Monthly/Daily Rest	Cost-per-£1,000
6.75%	6.5477	6.4851	5.6250
6.50%	6.3815	6.3198	5.4167
6.25%	6.2169	6.1562	5.2083
6.00%	6.0541	5.9945	5.0000
5.75%	5.8930	5.8347	4.7917
5.50%	5.7338	5.6768	4.5833
5.25%	5.5764	5.5209	4.3750
5.00%	5.4210	5.3670	4.1667
4.75%	5.2675	5.2152	3.9583
4.50%	5.1160	5.0655	3.7500
4.25%	4.9665	4.9180	3.5417
4.00%	4.8192	4.7727	3.3333
3.75%	4.6740	4.6296	3.1250
3.50%	4.5309	4.4889	2.9167
3.25%	4.3901	4.3504	2.7083
3.00%	4.2516	4.2143	2.5000
2.75%	4.1154	4.0806	2.2917
2.50%	3.9815	3.9493	2.0833
2.25%	3.8499	3.8205	1.8750
2.00%	3.7208	3.6942	1.6667
1.00%	3.2290	3.2140	0.8333

Appendix C – Help at hand

For further advice on any of the information given in this book, here are the contact addresses and telephone numbers of the organizations most able to help

Credit reference agencies

For a fee of £1 or £2, these agencies will supply information held on their files about you:

Equifax Europe (UK) Ltd
Consumer Affairs Department
Spectrum House
1A North Avenue
Clydebank
Glasgow G81 2DR
Tel: (0990) 783 783

Experian Ltd
Consumer Help Services
PO Box 40
Nottingham NG7 2SS
Tel: (0115) 976 8747

If you find any information that's incorrect on your credit file, contact your local Office of Fair Trading for a free leaflet entitled 'No Credit?'. This explains how to get your file corrected.

Getting advice and help

If you are having difficulties repaying your mortgage loan, or are in financial difficulty, contact your local Citizens Advice Bureau or money advice centre. You'll find their telephone numbers in your local telephone directory.

For advice and information on all forms of debt, contact:

National Debtline
Money Advice Services
318 Summer Lane
Birmingham B19 3RL
Tel: (0121) 359 8501

For details of local housing aid centres, contact:

Shelter Housing Services
88 Old Street
London EC1V 9HU
Tel: (0171) 505 2000

SHELTER Scotland
8 Hampton Terrace
Edinburgh EH12 5JD
Tel: (0131) 313 1550

Mortgage complaints

If you have a complaint against your mortgage lender, the first course of action is to write to your branch office, which has internal procedures for dealing with complaints. These escalate to the branch's head office if necessary. If your lender doesn't have a branch office, write to its head office.

If your complaint remains unresolved and the lender's internal procedures have been exhausted, there are three complaints bodies who can investigate mortgage complaints further:

Banking Ombudsman
70 Grays Inn Road
London WC1X 8NB
Tel: (0171) 404 9944
(The body that considers complaints against banks)

Building Societies Ombudsman
Millbank Tower
Millbank
London SW1P 4SX
Tel: (0171) 931 0044
(The body that considers complaints against building societies)

Chartered Institute of Arbitrators
24 Angel Gate
City Road
London EC1V 2RS
Tel: (0171) 837 4483
(The body that considers complaints against mortgage lenders that are neither banks nor building societies)

If your lender is not a member of the above schemes, contact your local Citizens Advice Bureau or Trading Standards Department for advice.

For complaints about an investment linked to a mortgage (for example, endowment, PEP or pension plan), contact:

Personal Investment Authority Ombudsman
Hertsmere House
Hertsmere Road
London E14 4AB
Tel: (0171) 216 0016

The Mortgage Code

For full details of the Mortgage Code and information on lenders and intermediaries, contact:

Council of Mortgage Lenders
3 Saville Row
London W1A 1AF
Tel: (0171) 440 2255

For a list of mortgage intermediaries who will help you choose a mortgage and who comply with the Mortgage Code, contact:

Mortgage Code Register of Intermediaries
Festival Way
Festival Park
Stoke-on-Trent
Staffordshire ST1 5TA
Tel: (01782) 216 300

Land Registry

If you want information relating to your property or anyone else's for that matter, contact:

District Land Registry Office
HM Land Registry
32 Lincoln's Inn Fields
London WC2A 3PH
Tel: (0171) 917 8888

Land Charges Registry
Burrington Way
Plymouth PL6 3LP
Tel: (01752) 779 831
(For land that is not registered)

Land Register
The Registers of Scotland
Meadowbank House
153 London Road
Edinburgh EH8 7AU
Tel: (0131) 659 6111

Appendix D – Delve deeper

Books, mags and Web sites that make for interesting reading

Books

If you're really interested in making mortgages a career, you'll need this publication:

The Institute of Financial Services (1997) *Practice, Products and Policy*, The Chartered Institute of Bankers

For practical advice to homebuyers in difficulty with mortgage repayments:

Moorhouse, P and Tait, G (1998) *Rights Guide for Home Owners*, 12th edn, CPAG Ltd and Shelter

Magazines

For detailed information on a wide range of mortgage topics and products, including interest rates, lending criteria, incentives and redemption periods, these magazines will help you out:

Moneyfacts, Moneyfacts Publications (tel: 01603 476 476)
What Mortgage?, Charterhouse Communications Ltd (tel: 0171 638 1916)
Your Mortgage, Brass Tacks Publishing Co (tel: 0171 833 5566)

Your Mortgage Hotline (tel: 0171 833 5566) provides details of current fixed and capped rate products on weekdays between 10 am and 1 pm.

Web sites

If you have access to the Internet, here are a few Web sites to check out for up-to-the-minute mortgage information:

The Slash Your Mortgage Web site at:
http://www.slash-mortgage.com

The Council of Mortgage Lenders Web site at: http://www.cml.co.uk

The Interactive Investor Web site at: http://www.iii.co.uk

The Moneyworld Web site at: http://www.moneyworld.co.uk

The Chase De Vere mortgage management Web site at:
http://www.cdvmortgage.co.uk

Glossary – Know how many beans make five

Your guide to the terms you're most likely to come across when remortgaging, and a few more besides. Bear in mind that they are not precise legal definitions

accounting year The year over which a lender operating the annual rest scheme calculates the mortgage loan interest on a variable rate mortgage.

additional security See mortgage insurance.

amenity Features that enhance a property's attractiveness but not essential to the property's use.

amortise The repayment method to satisfy a mortgage loan by regular capital and interest instalments.

annual mortgage statement A statement showing how much interest has been paid during the accounting year, as well as the remaining mortgage loan balance.

annual percentage rate (APR) The total cost of a mortgage stated as a yearly rate and includes items such as interest, mortgage insurance, and loan arrangement fee. It allows the fairest comparison of the terms offered by various lenders.

annuity-linked mortgage See reversion scheme.

apparent insolvency See bankruptcy.

arrangement fee A fee paid to a lender for processing a loan application. Also known as an application fee or booking fee.

asset Anything of monetary value owned by a person, such as land, personal property, bank accounts, share certificates, endowments, and so on.

assignment The transfer of a life policy used to repay an interest-only mortgage at the end of the mortgage term. The lender has the right to cash in the policy if the borrower defaults on the mortgage payment. The life assurance company must also inform the lender of lapsed payments or when the policy matures.

attorney A person legally entitled to act on another person's behalf.

bankrupt A person or organization owing more than their assets and deemed insolvent by a court proceeding. The lender has right to possession of the property, but will usually only exercise this right if the mortgage loan goes into arrears. Now more commonly known as 'apparent insolvency'.

bond An interest-bearing certificate of debt issued by a company that guarantees that the creditor will be repaid in full at a future date. The government also issues bonds, known as gilts.

booking fee See arrangement fee.

bridging loan A loan used to complete the purchase of a new home before the present home is sold.

broker A person or company that brings together borrowers and lenders and assists in negotiating contracts between them for a commission or fee.

building society A mutual organization owned by its members (savers and borrowers). Loans to borrowers were once funded solely from the money deposited by savers.

building warrant Permissions issued under local regulations that control design, construction, and materials used in construction. Building warrants are based on safety and health standards.

capital The amount borrowed or remaining unpaid on the mortgage loan on which interest is paid. The part of the monthly payment that reduces the remaining balance of a mortgage loan.

capital balance The outstanding balance of capital on a mortgage but does not include interest or any other charges.

capital reduction Any amount paid to reduce the capital balance of a loan before the scheduled due date. Payment in part or full may incur a redemption fee and is usually a percentage of the amount repaid. Also known as part redemption.

charge The legal right a lender has over a property, which allows the lender right of possession if the borrower defaults on the mortgage loan. See also legal charge.

clear title A title that is unencumbered and free of any legal questions as to ownership of the property. Any conditions revealed in a title search that may adversely affect the title cannot usually be removed except by court action.

common areas Parts of a building, land, and amenities belonging to and shared between owners. Common expenses of its operation and maintenance are also shared. Common areas include recreational facilities, as well as common corridors of buildings, parking areas and so on.

completion The date on which the mortgage contract is finalized and becomes legally binding. In Scotland, this is called 'settlement'.

compound interest Interest paid on an investment and its accrued interest.

condemnation A judgement that a building is not fit for use or is dangerous and must be demolished.

consent to mortgage form A form that must be completed by any occupier aged 17 and over and not participating in the mortgage. This document relinquishes the occupier's right of tenancy and gives the lender vacant possession if the mortgage loan is in default.

conveyance The legal transfer of ownership of freehold, leasehold or feudal land.

covenant A clause in a mortgage deed that obligates (positive covenant) or restricts (restrictive covenant) the owner and that, if breached, can result in repossession.

credit reference agency An organization that prepares files used by lenders to determine a potential borrower's credit worthiness.

credit scoring The system used by most lenders to assist in deciding the credit risk of a mortgage applicant.

creditor A person who is owed a financial obligation. In Scotland, this is the lender in a mortgage agreement.

debt Money that is owed that includes interest and incidental charges.

debtor A person who owes a financial obligation. In Scotland, this is the borrower in a mortgage agreement.

decreasing term assurance A type of term life insurance whereby the amount of cover decreases as the capital balance of a repayment mortgage decreases. Should the borrower die while the policy is in force, the mortgage loan is automatically satisfied by the insurer. See also level term assurance.

deed of postponement An agreement that allows the primary lender to take out a further charge on a property by deferring the priority of a secondary lender.

default Failure to make mortgage payments when they are due, or to comply with other requirements of the mortgage agreement. If the conditions haven't been met within a specified period, the lender can start court proceedings for possession.

default notice A formal written notice by a lender to a borrower that a legal action may be taken to recover payment of a debt or to repossess the property. It explains the nature of the breach, how the breach can be remedied, and the time limit for amendment. In Scotland, this is a 'calling up notice'.

defective title insurance Insurance that protects the lender or the borrower against the risk of another party claiming to own the property or to have rights over it.

deposit The sum of money that is put towards the financing of a mortgage loan. The larger the deposit, the less a mortgage insurance premium is charged.

depreciation A decline in the value of property often resulting in negative equity.

discharge The removal by the lender of the charge on the property when the mortgage loan has been repaid.

disposition See conveyance.

enforcement order An order issued by a local authority to compel compliance with local authority regulations. Usually issued when there's structural damage or when alterations have been made without planning consent.

equity The difference between the market value of the property and the amount still owed on the mortgage loan.

estate The sum total of all the property owned by someone at the time of death.

eviction The lawful expulsion of an occupant from his or her property for defaulting on the mortgage conditions.

exchange of contracts The point at which the seller and purchaser are committed to proceed with the sale of the property. In Scotland, this is known as 'conclusion of missives'.

feudal estate The chief form of land ownership in Scotland.

first charge A mortgage that is the primary security over a property.

foreclosure The legal process whereby a borrower in default of a mortgage loan forfeits the equity in the property on its sale. Foreclosure has almost ceased in this country.

freehold A form of ownership that gives almost absolute right of land and property. Freeholders can offer the land or property for rent to leaseholders.

full structural survey A full report on the structure, condition and value of a property by a qualified surveyor. Recommended for older homes, and is the most expensive type of survey. Also known as a full building survey.

gilts An interest-bearing certificate of debt issued by the government that guarantees that the creditor will be repaid in full at a future date. This is probably the safest investment and consequently has lower returns.

gross income Normal annual income, including regular or guaranteed overtime or bonuses, before taxes and any other deductions.

ground rent An amount of money paid for the use of land or property when the title is held as leasehold rather than freehold.

guarantor A person who guarantees that the mortgage loan will be repaid should the borrower default on payment of the mortgage loan. Both the borrower and the guarantor are equally responsible for the repayment.

homebuyer's report An inspection by a surveyor to evaluate the structural condition of a property. Less thorough than a full structural survey whereby major structural defects, woodworm, wood rot and damp are reported, but not the roof. Less expensive than a full structural survey. Also known as an intermediate survey.

income support mortgage interest (ISMI) The benefit paid to cover the interest payments on a mortgage loan when the borrower is unemployed. The qualifying period for mortgages taken out from 2 October 1995 is 39 weeks and the benefit is means tested.

initial interest rate The original interest rate of the mortgage at the start of the mortgage term.

interest The fee charged by a lender for borrowing money.

interest-only mortgage A mortgage that has monthly payments to repay only the interest owed on the loan over a stated term. Generally, a lump sum payment to repay the loan is due at the end of the term.

interest rate The rate of interest that's in force when the monthly payment is due.

joint and several liability Allows the lender to sue only one participant in a multi-participant mortgage to recover all sums due. This participant has the right of relief to seek fair contribution from the other participants.

joint tenancy A form of property ownership that gives each tenant equal and absolute rights to the property. In the event of death, the property passes to the surviving participant(s). In Scotland this is known as joint property.

Land Registry The organization responsible for land registration in England and Wales. Recorded details include property, proprietorship and charges. In Scotland, the organization is the Land Register of Scotland.

lease An agreement between the owner of a property and a tenant that defines the conditions under which the tenant can occupy the property for a specified period and rent.

leasehold A way of holding title to a property wherein the mortgagor does not actually own the property but rather has a recorded long-term lease on it.

legal charge The principal type of mortgage deed in England and Wales. In Scotland it is known as a standard security.

level term assurance A life insurance plan whereby the amount of cover remains the same throughout the life of the policy. Often used in conjunction with an interest-only mortgage. See also decreasing term assurance.

lien The right to retain possession of the borrower's property until the mortgage debt is repaid.

loan-to-value (LTV) ratio The relationship between the capital balance of the mortgage and the assessed value of the property.

lock-in See redemption period.

maturity The date on which the capital balance of a loan, life assurance policy or other financial plan becomes due and payable.

mortgage agreement A contract between lender and borrower that governs the mortgage loan and obligates the lender to make funds available to the borrower, and obligates the borrower to repay the loan over a specified period of time.

mortgage deed A legal document that pledges a property to the lender as security for payment of a mortgage loan.

mortgage indemnity policy (MIP) A contract that insures the lender against loss caused by a borrower's default on the mortgage loan. It is a single premium paid on behalf of the lender by the borrower. The insurer can recover its loss from the borrower under a legal process known as subrogation.

mortgage insurance A mortgage that is protected by a mortgage insurance policy. If the borrower is unable to make his or her mortgage payment through involuntary redundancy, accident or disability, the insurer pays the lender the monthly mortgage payment amount insured.

mortgage loan The total amount of capital owed on a mortgage before any payments are made.

mortgage offer A formal offer by a lender stating the terms under which it agrees to lend money to a homebuyer. It is an offer with conditions and is therefore not legally binding until formally accepted by the borrower. Also known as 'offer of advance'.

mortgage term The amount of time required to repay the mortgage loan, usually 25 years, though this can be extended or reduced.

mortgagee The lender in a mortgage agreement.

mortgagor The borrower in a mortgage agreement.

negative equity The circumstances whereby the total value of loans secured on a property exceeds the property's value.

notary public A public official, usually a solicitor, who is legally authorized to warrant and endorse documents such as affidavits.

offer of advance See mortgage offer.

part-redemption See capital reduction.

possession The legal right of a lender to call in the mortgage. The lender must seek a court order to obtain vacant possession. In Scotland, possession is known as 'calling up'.

possessory title Also known as 'squatters rights'. An occupier who registers this title with the Land Registry is granted absolute right to a property or land if the title is not challenged within 12 years. Absolute title is granted 15 years after registration.

power of sale The legal right of the lender to action the sale of a property to repay the mortgage debt. In Scotland, it is known as 'notice of default'.

principal See capital.

redemption payment The final lump sum payment that is made at maturity of an interest-only mortgage.

redemption penalty A fee that may be charged to a borrower who pays part or all of the mortgage loan before it is due. It is usually charged at three or six months' gross interest or a percentage of the amount of the mortgage loan.

redemption period The time period during which the lender guarantees an interest rate to a borrower. The lock-in also specifies the redemption penalty if the mortgage is paid off before the redemption period expires.

remortgaging The process of repaying one loan with the proceeds from a new loan using the same property as security. Also known as refinancing.

repayment mortgage A mortgage that has monthly payments to repay both the capital and interest on the loan over a stated term.

retention A condition whereby the lender retains part of the mortgage advance until suspensive conditions have been satisfied. This usually refers to the borrower making good the property. Home improvements may require a re-inspection report before funds are released.

reversion scheme A plan that enables older homeowners to release part or all of the equity in their homes from the sale of their property to a lender. The lender provides a lump sum from which an annuity is purchased (although not obligatory). Unlike home-equity plans, the annuity income is mortgage payment-free. When the borrower dies, the loan is repaid from the sale of the property.

search See title search.

second charge A secured loan that ranks subordinate to the first secured loan.

secured loan A loan that is supported by an asset that guarantees repayment of a loan.

security Assets such as title deeds, life policies and share certificates used as support for a mortgage loan. The lender has the right to sell the security if the loan is not repaid according to the terms of the mortgage agreement.

stage payments The method used to release funds to finance a self-build project. The lender makes payments to the builder at periodic intervals as the work progresses.

stamp duty A government tax on a property when the purchase price stated in the conveyance exceeds £60,000. The tax is payable on the transfer of ownership of the property.

standard security The only type of mortgage deed in Scotland. In England and Wales it is known as a legal charge.

sue on personal covenant The right of a lender to demand payment of the entire capital balance if a monthly payment is missed.

surrender value The amount of money an endowment policy yields when it is cashed in before reaching maturity. It generally takes about seven years before the amount paid in equals the surrender value.

survey A written report of the estimated value of a property prepared by a qualified valuer such as an architect or chartered surveyor. See also homebuyer's report, structural survey and valuation report.

term life assurance See level term assurance and decreasing term assurance.

tied agent Salespeople selling products and services on behalf of one company. Their financial advice is neither impartial nor independent.

title deed A legal document that proves a person's right to or ownership of a property.

title search A check of the title records to ensure that the seller is the legal owner of the property and that there are no liens or other claims outstanding.

transfer of ownership Any means by which the ownership of a property changes hands.

underwriting The process of evaluating a loan application to determine the risk involved for the lender. Underwriting involves an analysis of the borrower's creditworthiness and the quality of the property itself.

unsecured loan A loan that is not supported by an asset to guarantee repayment of a loan.

valuation report A report of a property's fair market value based on a valuer's assessment of the property. A valuation is always carried out by a new lender when remortgaging.

variable rate mortgage A mortgage that permits the lender to adjust its interest rate periodically, usually in line with the Bank of England's base lending rate.

Index